The Simple

Air Fryer

Cookbook for UK Beginners 2024

1900 Days Tasty, Effortless, and Affordable Recipes Book | Tips & Tricks for Perfect Air Frying, Grilling, and Baking in Under 30 Minutes

Sahar Rosendahl

Table of Contents

Introduction

Introducing the Air Fryer Cookbook: Your Ticket to Flavorful, Healthier Eating in the Fast Lane! Get ready to dive into a world where crispy delights meet guilt-free indulgence, perfectly tailored to the American lifestyle.

Imagine savoring crispy fries, juicy chicken wings, and crunchy snacks—all without the guilt of excess oil. With the Air Fryer Cookbook, these mouthwatering dishes are not just a dream; they're a reality waiting to be enjoyed, perfect for busy Americans craving delicious meals without the hassle.

But this cookbook isn't just about recipes; it's a culinary journey that celebrates the unique flavors and convenience of air frying. Say goodbye to greasy frying methods and hello to a healthier, yet equally satisfying alternative. With minimal to no oil, you'll achieve that crispy perfection without compromising on taste or texture, ideal for the fast-paced American lifestyle.

At the heart of our cookbook lies the Air Fryer—an innovation designed for modern living. Its dual cooking zones offer unmatched flexibility and efficiency, allowing you to prepare two distinct dishes simultaneously, without any flavor mingling. It's like having two air fryers in one, perfect for multitasking Americans who value convenience.

But that's not all! Our cookbook is your ultimate guide to mastering the art of air frying. Dive into essential techniques, learn optimal cooking temperatures, and discover how to elevate flavors using marinades, spices, and coatings. Plus, we'll share tips on proper maintenance to ensure your air fryer remains a kitchen essential for years to come.

So, are you ready to revolutionize your cooking experience? Let the Air Fryer Cookbook be your companion as we embark on a journey to healthier, flavorful eating, perfectly tailored to the American lifestyle. From quick weeknight dinners to indulgent weekend treats, we'll show you how to create delicious meals that fit seamlessly into your busy schedule.

Embrace the ease and convenience of air frying and let your taste buds soar!

Introducing the Air Fryer: A Modern Solution to Healthier, Crispy Cooking

Ever wondered how to enjoy crispy, delicious foods without the guilt of excess oil? Enter the air fryer—a revolutionary kitchen appliance that's changing the way we cook. But what exactly is an air fryer?

Think of it as your own personal chef, using hot air to circulate around your food, creating that perfect golden crispiness without drowning it in oil. It's like having a mini convection oven right on your countertop, ready to whip up your favorite dishes in a healthier way.

But air fryers aren't just about frying. They're versatile machines that can grill, roast, and bake too. From crispy chicken wings to tender vegetables and even decadent desserts, the possibilities are endless.

Now, let's talk about why air fryers are all the rage:

Healthier Cooking: By using little to no oil, air fryers offer a healthier alternative to traditional frying methods, perfect for those looking to watch their waistlines without sacrificing flavor.

Speed and Convenience: With simple controls and rapid cooking times, air fryers make meal prep a breeze. No more waiting for the oven to preheat or dealing with messy frying oil.

Crispy Texture: Air fryers deliver that satisfying crunch without the excess grease, giving you the crispy texture you crave without the guilt.

Easy Cleanup: Most air fryers come with removable, dishwasher-safe parts, making cleanup a cinch. Say goodbye to scrubbing greasy pans!

Space-Saving Design: Compact and sleek, air fryers take up minimal counter space, making them perfect for small kitchens or crowded countertops.

So, why wait? Join the air frying revolution and

discover a healthier, tastier way to enjoy your favorite foods. With an air fryer by your side, every meal is a crispy, guilt-free delight!

Tips for Air Fryer Beginners

Embarking on your air frying journey? Here are some handy tips to help you master your new kitchen gadget:

1. Preheat with Purpose: Just like warming up an oven, preheating your air fryer is key to achieving that perfect crisp. Give it a few minutes to heat up before adding your food for even cooking.

2. Mind the Gap: Avoid overcrowding the basket or tray. Leave some breathing room between food items to allow hot air to circulate evenly, ensuring everything cooks to crispy perfection.

3. Shake it Up: Midway through cooking, give the basket or tray a gentle shake to redistribute the food. This helps ensure all sides get that golden crunch you're craving.

4. Oil in Moderation: While you can skip the oil altogether, a light spritz can enhance flavor and texture. Opt for a spray bottle to apply a thin, even coat before cooking.

5. Temperature Trials: Every air fryer has its quirks, so don't be afraid to experiment with different temperatures and cooking times. Start with the recommended settings, then adjust to suit your taste.

6. Keep it Clean: To keep your air fryer in top condition, give it a wipe down after each use and follow the manufacturer's instructions for deep cleaning. A clean air fryer is a happy air fryer!

With these tips in your arsenal, you'll be whipping up crispy, delicious meals in your air fryer like a pro in no time. Happy cooking!

Caring for Your Air Fryer: Tips for Cleaning and Maintenance

1) Regular Wipe-downs: After each use, give your air fryer a quick wipe-down with a damp cloth or sponge to remove any food residue or grease. This prevents buildup and keeps your appliance looking clean.

2) Deep Cleaning Routine: Set aside time for a thorough cleaning of your air fryer every few weeks. Refer to the manufacturer's instructions for guidance on how to deep clean the interior and exterior components effectively.

3) Gentle Cleaning Agents: Opt for mild, non-abrasive cleaners when cleaning your air fryer. Harsh chemicals or abrasive scrubbers can damage the surfaces, so stick to gentle dish soap and a soft sponge or cloth.

4) Mindful Water Usage: Air fryers should never be submerged in water, as this can damage the electrical components. Instead, focus on cleaning the removable parts like the basket and tray separately under running water.

5) Proper Storage: When not in use, store your air fryer in a cool, dry place away from direct sunlight and heat sources. Avoid stacking heavy items on top of it, as this can cause damage or deformation.

6) Inspection and Replacement: Regularly inspect your air fryer for any signs of damage or wear. If you notice cracked parts, frayed cords, or malfunctioning components, replace them promptly to maintain optimal performance and safety.

By incorporating these cleaning and maintenance practices into your routine, you can ensure that your air fryer stays in top condition, prolonging its lifespan and ensuring delicious, crispy results with every use.

CHAPTER 1 Breakfast Delights

Three-Berry Dutch Pancake

Prep time: 10 minutes | Cook time: 12 to 16 minutes | Serves 4

- 2 egg whites
- 1 egg
- 60 g wholemeal plain flour plus 1 tablespoon cornflour
- 120 ml semi-skimmed milk
- 1 teaspoon pure vanilla extract
- 1 tablespoon unsalted butter, melted
- 235 g sliced fresh strawberries
- 120 g fresh blueberries
- 120 g fresh raspberries

1. In a medium bowl, use an eggbeater or hand mixer to quickly mix the egg whites, egg, flour, milk, and vanilla until well combined. 2. Use a pastry brush to grease the bottom of a baking pan with the melted butter. Immediately pour in the batter and put the basket back in the fryer. Bake at 170°C for 12 to 16 minutes, or until the pancake is puffed and golden brown. 3. Remove the pan from the air fryer; the pancake will fall. Top with the strawberries, blueberries, and raspberries. Serve immediately.

Honey-Apricot Muesli with Greek Yoghurt

Prep time: 10 minutes | Cook time: 30 minutes | Serves 6

- 235 g porridge oats
- 60 g dried apricots, diced
- 60 g almond slivers
- 60 g walnuts, chopped
- 60 g pumpkin seeds
- 60 to 80 ml honey, plus more for drizzling
- 1 tablespoon rapeseed oil
- 1 teaspoon ground cinnamon
- ¼ teaspoon ground nutmeg
- ¼ teaspoon salt
- 2 tablespoons sugar-free dark chocolate crisps

(optional)

- 700 ml fat-free natural yoghurt

1. Preheat the air fryer to 130°C. Line the air fryer basket with parchment paper. 2. In a large bowl, combine the oats, apricots, almonds, walnuts, pumpkin seeds, honey, rapeseed oil, cinnamon, nutmeg, and salt, mixing so that the honey, oil, and spices are well distributed. 3. Pour the mixture onto the parchment paper and spread it into an even layer. 4. Bake for 10 minutes, then shake or stir and spread back out into an even layer. Continue baking for 10 minutes more, then repeat the process of shaking or stirring the mixture. Bake for an additional 10 minutes before removing from the air fryer. 5. Allow the muesli to cool completely before stirring in the chocolate crisps (if using) and pouring into an airtight container for storage. 6. For each serving, top 120 ml Greek yoghurt with 80 ml muesli and a drizzle of honey, if needed.

Scotch Eggs

Prep time: 10 minutes | Cook time: 20 to 25 minutes | Serves 4

- 2 tablespoons flour, plus extra for coating
- 450 g banger meat
- 4 hard-boiled eggs, peeled
- 1 raw egg
- 1 tablespoon water
- Oil for misting or cooking spray
- Crumb Coating:
- 90 g breadcrumbs
- 90 g flour

1. Combine flour with banger meat and mix thoroughly. 2. Divide into 4 equal portions and mould each around a hard-boiled egg so the banger completely covers the egg. 3. In a small bowl, beat together the raw egg and water. 4. Dip banger-covered eggs in the remaining flour, then the egg mixture, then roll in the crumb coating. 5. Air fry at 180°C for 10 minutes. Spray eggs, turn, and spray other side. 6. Continue cooking for another 10 to 15 minutes or until banger is well done.

Quick and Easy Blueberry Muffins

Prep time: 10 minutes | Cook time: 12 minutes | Makes 8 muffins

- ◆ 160 g flour
- ◆ 96 g sugar
- ◆ 2 teaspoons baking powder
- ◆ ¼ teaspoon salt
- ◆ 80 ml rapeseed oil
- ◆ 1 egg
- ◆ 120 ml milk
- ◆ 160 g blueberries, fresh or frozen and thawed

1. Preheat the air fryer to 170°C. 2. In a medium bowl, stir together flour, sugar, baking powder, and salt. 3. In a separate bowl, combine oil, egg, and milk and mix well. 4. Add egg mixture to dry ingredients and stir just until moistened. 5. Gently stir in the blueberries. 6. Spoon batter evenly into parchment paper-lined muffin cups. 7. Put 4 muffin cups in air fryer basket and bake for 12 minutes or until tops spring back when touched lightly. 8. Repeat previous step to bake remaining muffins. 9. Serve immediately.

Cinnamon-Raisin Bagels

Prep time: 30 minutes | Cook time: 10 minutes | Makes 4 bagels

- ◆ Oil, for spraying
- ◆ 60 g raisins
- ◆ 120 g self-raising flour, plus more for dusting
- ◆ 235 ml natural yoghurt
- ◆ 1 teaspoon ground cinnamon
- ◆ 1 large egg

1. Line the air fryer basket with parchment and spray lightly with oil. 2. Place the raisins in a bowl of hot water and let sit for 10 to 15 minutes, until they have plumped. This will make them extra juicy. 3. In a large bowl, mix together the flour, yoghurt, and cinnamon with your hands or a large silicone spatula until a ball is formed. It will be quite sticky for a while. 4. Drain the raisins and gently work them into the ball of dough. 5. Place the dough on a lightly floured work surface and divide into 4 equal pieces. Roll each piece into an 8- or 9-inch-long rope and shape it into a circle, pinching the ends together to seal. 6. In a small bowl, whisk the egg. Brush the egg onto the tops of the dough. 7. Place the dough in the prepared basket. 8. Air fry at 180°C for 10 minutes. Serve immediately.

Egg in a Hole

Prep time: 5 minutes | Cook time: 5 minutes | Serves 1

- ◆ 1 slice bread
- ◆ 1 teaspoon butter, softened
- ◆ 1 egg
- ◆ Salt and pepper, to taste
- ◆ 1 tablespoon grated Cheddar cheese
- ◆ 2 teaspoons diced gammon

1. Preheat the air fryer to 170°C. Place a baking dish in the air fryer basket. 2. On a flat work surface, cut a hole in the center of the bread slice with a 2½-inch-diameter biscuit cutter. 3. Spread the butter evenly on each side of the bread slice and transfer to the baking dish. 4. Crack the egg into the hole and season as desired with salt and pepper. Scatter the grated cheese and diced gammon on top. 5. Bake in the preheated air fryer for 5 minutes until the bread is lightly browned and the egg is cooked to your preference. 6. Remove from the basket and serve hot.

Berry Muffins

Prep time: 15 minutes | Cook time: 12 to 17 minutes | Makes 8 muffins

- ◆ 160 g plus 1 tablespoon plain flour, divided
- ◆ 48 g granulated sugar
- ◆ 2 tablespoons light soft brown sugar
- ◆ 2 teaspoons baking powder
- ◆ 2 eggs
- ◆ 160 ml whole milk
- ◆ 80 ml neutral oil
- ◆ 235 g mixed fresh berries

1. In a medium bowl, stir together 315 g of flour, the granulated sugar, soft brown sugar, and baking powder until mixed well. 2. In a small bowl, whisk the eggs, milk, and oil until combined. Stir the egg mixture into the dry ingredients just until combined. 3. In another small bowl, toss the mixed berries with the remaining 1 tablespoon of flour until coated. Gently stir the berries into the batter. 4. Double up 16 foil muffin cups to make 8 cups. 5. Insert the crisper plate into the basket and the basket into the unit. Preheat the unit by selecting BAKE, setting the temperature to 160°C, and setting the time to 3 minutes. Select START/STOP to begin. 6. Once the unit is preheated, place 1 L into the basket and fill each three-quarters full with the batter. 7. Select BAKE, set the temperature to 160°C, and set the time

for 17 minutes. Select START/STOP to begin. 8. After about 12 minutes, check the muffins. If they spring back when lightly touched with your finger, they are done. If not, resume cooking. 9. When the cooking is done, transfer the muffins to a wire rack to cool. 10. Repeat steps 6, 7, and 8 with the remaining muffin cups and batter. 11. Let the muffins cool for 10 minutes before serving.

Bourbon Vanilla Eggy Bread

Prep time: 15 minutes | Cook time: 6 minutes | Serves 4

◆ 2 large eggs
◆ 2 tablespoons water
◆ 160 ml whole or semi-skimmed milk
◆ 1 tablespoon butter, melted
◆ 2 tablespoons bourbon
◆ 1 teaspoon vanilla extract
◆ 8 (1-inch-thick) French bread slices
◆ Cooking spray

1. Preheat the air fryer to 160°C. Line the air fryer basket with parchment paper and spray it with cooking spray. 2. Beat the eggs with the water in a shallow bowl until combined. Add the milk, melted butter, bourbon, and vanilla and stir to mix well. 3. Dredge 4 slices of bread in the batter, turning to coat both sides evenly. Transfer the bread slices onto the parchment paper. 4. Bake for 6 minutes until nicely browned. Flip the slices halfway through the cooking time. 5. Remove from the basket to a plate and repeat with the remaining 4 slices of bread. 6. Serve warm.

Cheddar Soufflés

Prep time: 15 minutes | Cook time: 12 minutes | Serves 4

◆ 3 large eggs, whites and yolks separated
◆ ¼ teaspoon cream of tartar
◆ 120 g grated mature Cheddar cheese
◆ 85 g soft cheese, softened

1. In a large bowl, beat egg whites together with cream of tartar until soft peaks form, about 2 minutes. 2. In a separate medium bowl, beat egg yolks, Cheddar, and soft cheese together until frothy, about 1 minute. Add egg yolk mixture to whites, gently folding until combined. 3. Pour mixture evenly into four ramekins greased with cooking spray. Place ramekins into air fryer basket. Adjust the temperature to 180°C and bake for 12 minutes. Eggs will be browned on the top and firm in the center

when done. Serve warm.

Apple Cider Doughnut Holes

Prep time: 10 minutes | Cook time: 6 minutes | Makes 10 mini doughnuts

◆ Doughnut Holes:
◆ 175 g plain flour
◆ 2 tablespoons granulated sugar
◆ 2 teaspoons baking powder
◆ 1 teaspoon baking soda
◆ ½ teaspoon coarse or flaky salt
◆ Pinch of freshly grated nutmeg
◆ 60 ml plus 2 tablespoons buttermilk, chilled
◆ 2 tablespoons apple cider or apple juice, chilled
◆ 1 large egg, lightly beaten
◆ Vegetable oil, for brushing
◆ Glaze:
◆ 96 g icing sugar
◆ 2 tablespoons unsweetened apple sauce
◆ ¼ teaspoon vanilla extract
◆ Pinch of coarse or flaky salt

1. Make the doughnut holes: In a bowl, whisk together the flour, granulated sugar, baking powder, baking soda, salt, and nutmeg until smooth. Add the buttermilk, cider, and egg and stir with a small rubber spatula or spoon until the dough just comes together. 2. Using a 28 g ice cream scoop or 2 tablespoons, scoop and drop 10 balls of dough into the air fryer basket, spaced evenly apart, and brush the tops lightly with oil. Air fry at 180°C until the doughnut holes are golden brown and fluffy, about 6 minutes. Transfer the doughnut holes to a wire rack to cool completely. 3. Make the glaze: In a small bowl, stir together the icing sugar, apple sauce, vanilla, and salt until smooth. 4. Dip the tops of the doughnuts holes in the glaze, then let stand until the glaze sets before serving. If you're impatient and want warm doughnuts, have the glaze ready to go while the doughnuts cook, then use the glaze as a dipping sauce for the warm doughnuts, fresh out of the air fryer.

Banger and Cheese Balls

Prep time: 10 minutes | Cook time: 12 minutes | Makes 16 balls

◆ 450 g pork banger meat, removed from casings
◆ 120 g grated Cheddar cheese
◆ 30 g full-fat soft cheese, softened

◆ 1 large egg

1. Mix all ingredients in a large bowl. Form into sixteen (1-inch) balls. Place the balls into the air fryer basket. 2. Adjust the temperature to 200°C and air fry for 12 minutes. 3. Shake the basket two or three times during cooking. Banger balls will be browned on the outside and have an internal temperature of at least 64°C when completely cooked. 4. Serve warm.

Bacon, Cheese, and Avocado Melt

Prep time: 5 minutes | Cook time: 3 to 5 minutes | Serves 2

◆ 1 avocado

◆ 4 slices cooked bacon, chopped

◆ 2 tablespoons tomato salsa

◆ 1 tablespoon double cream

◆ 60 g grated Cheddar cheese

1. Preheat the air fryer to 200°C. 2. Slice the avocado in half lengthwise and remove the stone. To ensure the avocado halves do not roll in the basket, slice a thin piece of skin off the base. 3. In a small bowl, combine the bacon, tomato salsa, and cream. Divide the mixture between the avocado halves and top with the cheese. 4. Place the avocado halves in the air fryer basket and air fry for 3 to 5 minutes until the cheese has melted and begins to brown. Serve warm.

Buffalo Chicken Breakfast Muffins

Prep time: 7 minutes | Cook time: 13 to 16 minutes | Serves 10

◆ 170 g grated cooked chicken

◆ 85 g blue cheese, crumbled

◆ 2 tablespoons unsalted butter, melted

◆ 80 ml Buffalo hot sauce, such as Frank's RedHot

◆ 1 teaspoon minced garlic

◆ 6 large eggs

◆ Sea salt and freshly ground black pepper, to taste

◆ Avocado oil spray

1. In a large bowl, stir together the chicken, blue cheese, melted butter, hot sauce, and garlic. 2. In a medium bowl or large liquid measuring cup, beat the eggs. Season with salt and pepper. 3. Spray 10 silicone muffin cups with oil. Divide the chicken mixture among the cups, and pour the egg mixture over top. 4. Place the cups in the air fryer and set to 150°C. Bake for 13 to 16 minutes, until the muffins are set and cooked through.

(Depending on the size of your air fryer, you may need to cook the muffins in batches.)

Turkey Breakfast Banger Patties

Prep time: 5 minutes | Cook time: 10 minutes | Serves 4

◆ 1 tablespoon chopped fresh thyme

◆ 1 tablespoon chopped fresh sage

◆ 1¼ teaspoons coarse or flaky salt

◆ 1 teaspoon chopped fennel seeds

◆ ¾ teaspoon smoked paprika

◆ ½ teaspoon onion granules

◆ ½ teaspoon garlic powder

◆ ⅛ teaspoon crushed red pepper flakes

◆ ⅛ teaspoon freshly ground black pepper

◆ 450 g lean turkey mince

◆ 120 g finely minced sweet apple (peeled)

1. Thoroughly combine the thyme, sage, salt, fennel seeds, paprika, onion granules, garlic powder, red pepper flakes, and black pepper in a medium bowl. 2. Add the turkey mince and apple and stir until well incorporated. Divide the mixture into 8 equal portions and shape into patties with your hands, each about ¼ inch thick and 3 inches in diameter. 3. Preheat the air fryer to 200°C. 4. Place the patties in the air fryer basket in a single layer. You may need to work in batches to avoid overcrowding. 5. Air fry for 5 minutes. Flip the patties and air fry for 5 minutes, or until the patties are nicely browned and cooked through. 6. Remove from the basket to a plate and repeat with the remaining patties. 7. Serve warm.

Pancake for Two

Prep time: 5 minutes | Cook time: 30 minutes | Serves 2

◆ 120 g blanched finely ground almond flour

◆ 2 tablespoons granular erythritol

◆ 1 tablespoon salted butter, melted

◆ 1 large egg

◆ 80 ml unsweetened almond milk

◆ ½ teaspoon vanilla extract

1. In a large bowl, mix all ingredients together, then pour half the batter into an ungreased round nonstick baking dish. 2. Place dish into air fryer basket. Adjust the temperature to 160°C and bake for 15 minutes. The pancake will be golden brown on top and firm, and a toothpick inserted in the center

will come out clean when done. Repeat with remaining batter. 3. Slice in half in dish and serve warm.

Meritage Eggs

Prep time: 5 minutes | Cook time: 8 minutes | Serves 2

- 2 teaspoons unsalted butter (or coconut oil for dairy-free), for greasing the ramekins
- 4 large eggs
- 2 teaspoons chopped fresh thyme
- ½ teaspoon fine sea salt
- ¼ teaspoon ground black pepper
- 2 tablespoons double cream (or unsweetened, unflavoured almond milk for dairy-free)
- 3 tablespoons finely grated Parmesan cheese (or chive soft cheese style spread, softened, for dairy-free)
- Fresh thyme leaves, for garnish (optional)

1. Preheat the air fryer to 200°C. Grease two (110 g) ramekins with the butter. 2. Crack 2 eggs into each ramekin and divide the thyme, salt, and pepper between the ramekins. Pour 1 tablespoon of the double cream into each ramekin. Sprinkle each ramekin with 1½ tablespoons of the Parmesan cheese. 3. Place the ramekins in the air fryer and bake for 8 minutes for soft-cooked yolks (longer if you desire a harder yolk). 4. Garnish with a sprinkle of ground black pepper and thyme leaves, if desired. Best served fresh.

Spinach and Bacon Roll-ups

Prep time: 5 minutes | Cook time: 8 to 9 minutes | Serves 4

- 4 wheat maize wraps (6- or 7-inch size)
- 4 slices Swiss cheese
- 235 g baby spinach leaves
- 4 slices turkey bacon
- Special Equipment:
- 4 cocktail sticks, soak in water for at least 30 minutes

1. Preheat the air fryer to 200°C. 2. On a clean work surface, top each tortilla with one slice of cheese and 60 ml spinach, then tightly roll them up. 3. Wrap each tortilla with a strip of turkey bacon and secure with a toothpick. 4. Arrange the roll-ups in the air fryer basket, leaving space between each roll-up. 5. Air fry for 4 minutes. Flip the roll-ups with tongs and rearrange them for more even cooking. Air fry for another 4 to 5 minutes until the bacon is crisp. 6. Rest for 5 minutes and remove the cocktail sticks before serving.

Double-Dipped Mini Cinnamon Biscuits

Prep time: 15 minutes | Cook time: 13 minutes | Makes 8 biscuits

- 240g blanched almond flour
- 60 g powdered sweetener
- 1 teaspoon baking powder
- ½ teaspoon fine sea salt
- 60 g plus 2 tablespoons (¾ stick) very cold unsalted butter
- 60 ml unsweetened, unflavoured almond milk
- 1 large egg
- 1 teaspoon vanilla extract
- 3 teaspoons ground cinnamon
- Glaze:
- 60 g powdered sweetener
- 60 ml double cream or unsweetened, unflavoured almond milk

1. Preheat the air fryer to 180°C. Line a pie dish that fits into your air fryer with parchment paper. 2. In a medium-sized bowl, mix together the almond flour, sweetener (if powdered; do not add liquid sweetener), baking powder, and salt. Cut the butter into ½-inch squares, then use a hand mixer to work the butter into the dry ingredients. When you are done, the mixture should still have chunks of butter. 3. In a small bowl, whisk together the almond milk, egg, and vanilla extract (if using liquid sweetener, add it as well) until blended. Using a fork, stir the wet ingredients into the dry ingredients until large clumps form. Add the cinnamon and use your hands to swirl it into the dough. 4. Form the dough into sixteen 1-inch balls and place them on the prepared pan, spacing them about ½ inch apart. (If you're using a smaller air fryer, work in batches if necessary.) Bake in the air fryer until golden, 10 to 13 minutes. Remove from the air fryer and let cool on the pan for at least 5 minutes. 5. While the biscuits bake, make the glaze: Place the powdered sweetener in a small bowl and slowly stir in the double cream with a fork. 6. When the biscuits have cooled somewhat, dip the tops into the glaze, allow it to dry a bit, and then dip again for a thick glaze. 7. Serve warm or at room temperature. Store unglazed biscuits in an airtight container in the refrigerator for up to 3 days or in the freezer for up to a month. Reheat in a preheated 180°C air fryer for 5 minutes, or until warmed

through, and dip in the glaze as instructed above.

Egg and Bacon Muffins

Prep time: 5 minutes | Cook time: 15 minutes | Serves 1

- 2 eggs
- Salt and ground black pepper, to taste
- 1 tablespoon green pesto
- 85 g grated Cheddar cheese
- 140 g cooked bacon
- 1 spring onion, chopped

1. Preheat the air fryer to 180ºC. Line a cupcake tin with parchment paper. 2. Beat the eggs with pepper, salt, and pesto in a bowl. Mix in the cheese. 3. Pour the eggs into the cupcake tin and top with the bacon and spring onion. 4. Bake in the preheated air fryer for 15 minutes, or until the egg is set. 5. Serve immediately.

Banger Egg Cup

Prep time: 10 minutes | Cook time: 15 minutes | Serves 6

- 340 g pork banger, removed from casings
- 6 large eggs
- ½ teaspoon salt
- ¼ teaspoon ground black pepper
- ½ teaspoon crushed red pepper flakes

1. Place banger in six 4-inch ramekins (about 60 g per ramekin) greased with cooking oil. Press banger down to cover bottom and about ½-inch up the sides of ramekins. Crack one egg into each ramekin and sprinkle evenly with salt, black pepper, and red pepper flakes. 2. Place ramekins into air fryer basket. Adjust the temperature to 180ºC and set the timer for 15 minutes. Egg cups will be done when banger is fully cooked to at least 64ºC and the egg is firm. Serve warm.

Jalapeño and Bacon Breakfast Pizza

Prep time: 5 minutes | Cook time: 10 minutes | Serves 2

- 235 ml grated Cheddar cheese
- 30 g soft cheese, broken into small pieces
- 4 slices cooked bacon, chopped
- 60 g chopped pickled jalapeños
- 1 large egg, whisked
- ¼ teaspoon salt

1. Place Mozzarella in a single layer on the bottom of an ungreased round nonstick baking dish. Scatter soft cheese pieces, bacon, and jalapeños over Mozzarella, then pour egg evenly around baking dish. 2. Sprinkle with salt and place into air fryer basket. Adjust the temperature to 170ºC and bake for 10 minutes. When cheese is brown and egg is set, pizza will be done. 3. Let cool on a large plate 5 minutes before serving.

Portobello Eggs Benedict

Prep time: 10 minutes | Cook time: 10 to 14 minutes | Serves 2

- 1 tablespoon rapeseed oil
- 2 cloves garlic, minced
- ¼ teaspoon dried thyme
- 2 portobello mushrooms, stems removed and gills scraped out
- 2 vine tomatoes, halved lengthwise
- Salt and freshly ground black pepper, to taste
- 2 large eggs
- 2 tablespoons grated Pecorino Romano cheese
- 1 tablespoon chopped fresh parsley, for garnish
- 1 teaspoon truffle oil (optional)

1. Preheat the air fryer to 200ºC. 2. In a small bowl, combine the rapeseed oil, garlic, and thyme. Brush the mixture over the mushrooms and tomatoes until thoroughly coated. Season to taste with salt and freshly ground black pepper. 3. Arrange the vegetables, cut side up, in the air fryer basket. Crack an egg into the center of each mushroom and sprinkle with cheese. Air fry for 10 to 14 minutes until the vegetables are tender and the whites are firm. When cool enough to handle, coarsely chop the tomatoes and place on top of the eggs. Scatter parsley on top and drizzle with truffle oil, if desired, just before serving.

Bacon and Spinach Egg Muffins

Prep time: 7 minutes | Cook time: 12 to 14 minutes | Serves 6

- 6 large eggs
- 60 ml double (whipping) cream
- ½ teaspoon sea salt
- ¼ teaspoon freshly ground black pepper
- ¼ teaspoon cayenne pepper (optional)
- 180 g frozen chopped spinach, thawed and drained
- 4 strips cooked bacon, crumbled
- 60 g grated Cheddar cheese

1. In a large bowl (with a spout if you have one), whisk together

the eggs, double cream, salt, black pepper, and cayenne pepper (if using). 2. Divide the spinach and bacon among 6 silicone muffin cups. Place the muffin cups in your air fryer basket. 3. Divide the egg mixture among the muffin cups. Top with the cheese. 4. Set the air fryer to 150ºC. Bake for 12 to 14 minutes, until the eggs are set and cooked through.

Quesadillas

Prep time: 10 minutes | Cook time: 15 minutes | Serves 4

◆ 4 eggs

◆ 2 tablespoons skimmed milk

◆ Salt and pepper, to taste

◆ Oil for misting or cooking spray

◆ 4 wheat maize wraps

◆ 4 tablespoons tomato salsa

◆ 60 g Cheddar cheese, grated

◆ ½ small avocado, peeled and thinly sliced

1. Preheat the air fryer to 130ºC. 2. Beat together eggs, milk, salt, and pepper. 3. Spray a baking pan lightly with cooking spray and add egg mixture. 4. Bake for 8 to 9 minutes, stirring every 1 to 2 minutes, until eggs are scrambled to your liking. Remove and set aside. 5. Spray one side of each maize wrap with oil or cooking spray. Flip over. 6. Divide eggs, tomato salsa, cheese, and avocado among the maize wraps, covering only half of each maize wrap. 7. Fold each maize wrap in half and press down lightly. 8. Place 2 maize wraps in air fryer basket and air fry at 200ºC for 3 minutes or until cheese melts and outside feels slightly crispy. Repeat with remaining two maize wraps. 9. Cut each cooked maize wrap into halves or thirds.

Egg White Cups

Prep time: 10 minutes | Cook time: 15 minutes | Serves 4

◆ 475 ml 100% liquid egg whites

◆ 3 tablespoons salted butter, melted

◆ ¼ teaspoon salt

◆ ¼ teaspoon onion granules

◆ ½ medium plum tomato, cored and diced

◆ 120 g chopped fresh spinach leaves

1. In a large bowl, whisk egg whites with butter, salt, and onion granules. Stir in tomato and spinach, then pour evenly into four ramekins greased with cooking spray. 2. Place ramekins into air fryer basket. Adjust the temperature to 150ºC and bake for 15 minutes. Eggs will be fully cooked and firm in the center when done. Serve warm.

CHAPTER 2 Easy Daily Favourites

Fish and Vegetable Tacos

Prep time: 15 minutes | Cook time: 9 to 12 minutes | Serves 4

- 450 g white fish fillets, such as sole or cod
- 2 teaspoons olive oil
- 3 tablespoons freshly squeezed lemon juice, divided
- 350 g chopped red cabbage
- 1 large carrot, grated
- 120 ml low-salt salsa
- 80 ml low-fat Greek yoghurt
- 4 soft low-salt wholemeal maize wraps

1. Brush the fish with the olive oil and sprinkle with 1 tablespoon of lemon juice. 2.Air fry in the air fryer basket at 200°C for 9 to 12 minutes, or until the fish just flakes when tested with a fork. 3.Meanwhile, in a medium bowl, stir together the remaining 2 tablespoons of lemon juice, the red cabbage, carrot, salsa, and yoghurt. 4.When the fish is cooked, remove it from the air fryer basket and break it up into large pieces. 5.Offer the fish, maize wraps, and the cabbage mixture, and let each person assemble a taco.

Bacon-Wrapped Hot Dogs

Prep time: 5 minutes | Cook time: 10 minutes | Serves 4

- Oil, for spraying
- 4 bacon rashers
- 4 hot dog bangers
- 4 hot dog rolls
- Toppings of choice

1. Line the air fryer basket with parchment and spray lightly with oil. 2.Wrap a strip of bacon tightly around each hot dog, taking care to cover the tips so they don't get too crispy. 3.Secure with a toothpick at each end to keep the bacon from shrinking. 4.Place the hot dogs in the prepared basket. 5.Air fry at 190°C for 8 to 9 minutes, depending on how crispy you like the bacon. For extra-crispy, cook the hot dogs at 200°C for 6 to 8 minutes. 6.Place the hot dogs in the buns, return them to the air fryer, and cook for another 1 to 2 minutes, or until the buns are warm. 7.Add your desired toppings and serve.

Personal Cauliflower Pizzas

Prep time: 10 minutes | Cook time: 25 minutes | Serves 2

- 1 (340 g) bag frozen riced cauliflower
- 75 g shredded Mozzarella cheese
- 15 g almond flour
- 20 g Parmesan cheese
- 1 large egg
- ½ teaspoon salt
- 1 teaspoon garlic powder
- 1 teaspoon dried oregano
- 4 tablespoons no-sugar-added marinara sauce, divided
- 110 g fresh Mozzarella, chopped, divided
- 140 g cooked chicken breast, chopped, divided
- 100 g chopped cherry tomatoes, divided
- 5 g fresh baby rocket, divided

1. Preheat the air fryer to 200°C. Cut 4 sheets of parchment paper to fit the basket of the air fryer. Brush with olive oil and set aside. 2. In a large glass bowl, microwave the cauliflower according to package directions. Place the cauliflower on a clean towel, draw up the sides, and squeeze tightly over a sink to remove the excess moisture. Return the cauliflower to the bowl and add the shredded Mozzarella along with the almond flour, Parmesan, egg, salt, garlic powder, and oregano. Stir until thoroughly combined. 3. Divide the dough into two equal portions. Place one piece of dough on the prepared parchment paper and pat gently into a thin, flat disk 7 to 8 inches in diameter. Air fry for 15 minutes until the crust begins to brown. Let cool for 5 minutes. 4. Transfer the parchment paper with the crust on top to a baking sheet. Place a second sheet of parchment paper over the crust. While holding the edges of both sheets together, carefully lift the crust off the baking sheet, flip it, and place it back in the air fryer basket. The new sheet of parchment paper is now on the bottom. Remove the top piece of paper and air fry the crust for another 15 minutes until the top begins to brown. Remove the basket from the air fryer. 5. Spread 2 tablespoons of the marinara sauce on top of the crust, followed by half the fresh Mozzarella, chicken, cherry tomatoes,

and rocket. Air fry for 5 to 10 minutes longer, until the cheese is melted and beginning to brown. Remove the pizza from the oven and let it sit for 10 minutes before serving. Repeat with the remaining ingredients to make a second pizza.

Veggie Tuna Melts

Prep time: 15 minutes | Cook time: 7 to 11 minutes | Serves 4

- ◆ 2 low-salt wholemeal English muffins, split
- ◆ 1 (170 g) tin chunk light low-salt tuna, drained
- ◆ 235 g shredded carrot
- ◆ 80 g chopped mushrooms
- ◆ 2 spring onions, white and green parts, sliced
- ◆ 80 ml fat-free Greek yoghurt
- ◆ 2 tablespoons low-salt wholegrain mustard
- ◆ 2 slices low-salt low-fat Swiss cheese, halved

1. Place the English muffin halves in the air fryer basket. 2.Air fry at 170°C for 3 to 4 minutes, or until crisp. Remove from the basket and set aside. 3.In a medium bowl, thoroughly mix the tuna, carrot, mushrooms, spring onions, yoghurt, and mustard. 4.Top each half of the muffins with one-fourth of the tuna mixture and a half slice of Swiss cheese. 5.Air fry for 4 to 7 minutes, or until the tuna mixture is hot and the cheese melts and starts to brown. 6.Serve immediately.

Fried Green Tomatoes

Prep time: 15 minutes | Cook time: 6 to 8 minutes | Serves 4

- ◆ 4 medium green tomatoes
- ◆ 50 g plain flour
- ◆ 2 egg whites
- ◆ 60 ml almond milk
- ◆ 235 g ground almonds
- ◆ 120 g Japanese breadcrumbs
- ◆ 2 teaspoons olive oil
- ◆ 1 teaspoon paprika
- ◆ 1 clove garlic, minced

1. Rinse the tomatoes and pat dry. 2.Cut the tomatoes into ½-inch slices, discarding the thinner ends. Put the flour on a plate. 3.In a shallow bowl, beat the egg whites with the almond milk until frothy. 4.And on another plate, combine the almonds, breadcrumbs, olive oil, paprika, and garlic and mix well. 5.Dip the tomato slices into the flour, then into the egg white mixture, then into the almond mixture to coat. 6.Place four of the coated

tomato slices in the air fryer basket. 7.Air fry at 200°C for 6 to 8 minutes or until the tomato coating is crisp and golden brown. 8.Repeat with remaining tomato slices and serve immediately.

Pork Stuffing Meatballs

Prep time: 10 minutes | Cook time: 12 minutes | Makes 35 meatballs

- ◆ Oil, for spraying
- ◆ 680 g finely chopped pork
- ◆ 120 g breadcrumbs
- ◆ 120 ml milk
- ◆ 60 g finely chopped onion
- ◆ 1 large egg
- ◆ 1 tablespoon dried rosemary
- ◆ 1 tablespoon dried thyme
- ◆ 1 teaspoon salt
- ◆ 1 teaspoon ground black pepper
- ◆ 1 teaspoon finely chopped fresh parsley

1. Line the air fryer basket with parchment and spray lightly with oil. 2.In a large bowl, mix together the finely chopped pork, breadcrumbs, milk, onion, egg, rosemary, thyme, salt, black pepper, and parsley. 3.Roll about 2 tablespoons of the mixture into a ball. 4.Repeat with the rest of the mixture. You should have 30 to 35 meatballs. 5.Place the meatballs in the prepared basket in a single layer, leaving space between each one. You may need to work in batches, depending on the size of your air fryer. 6.Air fry at 200°C for 10 to 12 minutes, flipping after 5 minutes, or until golden brown and the internal temperature reaches 72°C.

Cheesy Baked Coarse Cornmeal

Prep time: 10 minutes | Cook time: 12 minutes | Serves 6

- ◆ 180 ml hot water
- ◆ 2 (28 g) packages instant grits
- ◆ 1 large egg, beaten
- ◆ 1 tablespoon melted butter
- ◆ 2 cloves garlic, minced
- ◆ ½ to 1 teaspoon red pepper flakes
- ◆ 235 g shredded Cheddar cheese or jalapeño Jack cheese

1. Preheat the air fryer to 200°C. 2.In a baking tray, combine the water, coarse cornmeal, egg, butter, garlic, and red pepper flakes. Stir until well combined. 3.Stir in the shredded cheese.

4.Place the pan in the air fryer basket and air fry for 12 minutes, or until the coarse cornmeal have cooked through and a knife inserted near the centre comes out clean. 5.Let stand for 5 minutes before serving.

Cheesy Potato Patties

Prep time: 5 minutes | Cook time: 10 minutes | Serves 8

- ◆ 900 g white potatoes
- ◆ 120 g finely chopped spring onions
- ◆ ½ teaspoon freshly ground black pepper, or more to taste
- ◆ 1 tablespoon fine sea salt
- ◆ ½ teaspoon hot paprika
- ◆ 475 g shredded Colby or Monterey Jack cheese
- ◆ 60 ml rapeseed oil
- ◆ 235 g crushed crackers

1. Preheat the air fryer to 180ºC. Boil the potatoes until soft. 2.Dry them off and peel them before mashing thoroughly, leaving no lumps. 3.Combine the mashed potatoes with spring onions, pepper, salt, paprika, and cheese. 4.Mould the mixture into balls with your hands and press with your palm to flatten them into patties. 5.In a shallow dish, combine the rapeseed oil and crushed crackers. 6.Coat the patties in the crumb mixture. 7.Bake the patties for about 10 minutes, in multiple batches if necessary. 8.Serve hot.

Baked Halloumi with Greek Salsa

Prep time: 15 minutes | Cook time: 6 minutes | Serves 4

- ◆ Salsa:
- ◆ 1 small shallot, finely diced
- ◆ 3 garlic cloves, minced
- ◆ 2 tablespoons fresh lemon juice
- ◆ 2 tablespoons extra-virgin olive oil
- ◆ 1 teaspoon freshly cracked black pepper
- ◆ Pinch of rock salt
- ◆ 120 ml finely diced English cucumber
- ◆ 1 plum tomato, deseeded and finely diced
- ◆ 2 teaspoons chopped fresh parsley
- ◆ 1 teaspoon snipped fresh dill
- ◆ 1 teaspoon snipped fresh oregano
- ◆ Cheese:
- ◆ 227 g Halloumi cheese, sliced into ½-inch-thick

pieces
- ◆ 1 tablespoon extra-virgin olive oil

1. Preheat the air fryer to 192ºC. 2. For the salsa: Combine the shallot, garlic, lemon juice, olive oil, pepper, and salt in a medium bowl. Add the cucumber, tomato, parsley, dill, and oregano. Toss gently to combine; set aside. 3. For the cheese: Place the cheese slices in a medium bowl. Drizzle with the olive oil. Toss gently to coat. 4. Arrange the cheese in a single layer in the air fryer basket. Bake for 6 minutes. 5. Divide the cheese among four serving plates. Top with the salsa and serve immediately.

Air Fried Shishito Peppers

Prep time: 5 minutes | Cook time: 5 minutes | Serves 4

- ◆ 230 g shishito or Padron peppers (about 24)
- ◆ 1 tablespoon olive oil
- ◆ Coarse sea salt, to taste
- ◆ Lemon wedges, for serving
- ◆ Cooking spray

1. Preheat the air fryer to 200ºC. 2.Spritz the air fryer basket with cooking spray. 3.Toss the peppers with olive oil in a large bowl to coat well. Arrange the peppers in the preheated air fryer. 4.Air fryer for 5 minutes or until blistered and lightly charred. Shake the basket and sprinkle the peppers with salt halfway through the cooking time. 5.Transfer the peppers onto a plate and squeeze the lemon wedges on top before serving.

Easy Devils on Horseback

Prep time: 5 minutes | Cook time: 7 minutes | Serves 12

- ◆ 24 small pitted prunes (128 g)
- ◆ 60 g crumbled blue cheese, divided
- ◆ 8 slices middle bacon, cut crosswise into thirds

1. Preheat the air fryer to 200ºC. 2.Halve the prunes lengthwise, but don't cut them all the way through. 3.Place ½ teaspoon of cheese in the centre of each prune. 4.Wrap a piece of bacon around each prune and secure the bacon with a toothpick. 5.Working in batches, arrange a single layer of the prunes in the air fryer basket. 6.Air fry for about 7 minutes, flipping halfway, until the bacon is cooked through and crisp. 7.Let cool slightly and serve warm.

Scalloped Veggie Mix

Prep time: 10 minutes | Cook time: 15 minutes | Serves 4

- 1 Yukon Gold or other small white potato, thinly sliced
- 1 small sweet potato, peeled and thinly sliced
- 1 medium carrot, thinly sliced
- 60 g minced onion
- 3 garlic cloves, minced
- 180 ml 2 percent milk
- 2 tablespoons cornflour
- ½ teaspoon dried thyme

1. Preheat the air fryer to 190°C. 2.In a baking tray, layer the potato, sweet potato, carrot, onion, and garlic. 3.In a small bowl, whisk the milk, cornflour, and thyme until blended. 4.Pour the milk mixture evenly over the vegetables in the pan. Bake for 15 minutes. 5.Check the casserole—it should be golden brown on top, and the vegetables should be tender. 6.Serve immediately.

Baked Cheese Sandwich

Prep time: 5 minutes | Cook time: 8 minutes | Serves 2

- 2 tablespoons mayonnaise
- 4 thick slices sourdough bread
- 4 thick slices Brie cheese
- 8 slices hot capicola or prosciutto

1. Preheat the air fryer to 180°C. 2.Spread the mayonnaise on one side of each slice of bread. 3.Place 2 slices of bread in the air fryer basket, mayonnaise-side down. 4.Place the slices of Brie and capicola on the bread and cover with the remaining two slices of bread, mayonnaise-side up. 5.Bake for 8 minutes, or until the cheese has melted. 6.Serve immediately.

Sweet Maize and Carrot Fritters

Prep time: 10 minutes | Cook time: 8 to 11 minutes | Serves 4

- 1 medium-sized carrot, grated
- 1 brown onion, finely chopped
- 4 ounces (113 g) canned sweet maize kernels, drained
- 1 teaspoon sea salt flakes
- 1 tablespoon chopped fresh coriander

- 1 medium-sized egg, whisked
- 2 tablespoons plain milk
- 1 cup grated Parmesan cheese
- ¼ cup flour
- ⅓ teaspoon baking powder
- ⅓ teaspoon sugar
- Cooking spray

1. Preheat the air fryer to 350°F (177°C). 2. Place the grated carrot in a colander and press down to squeeze out any excess moisture. Dry it with a paper towel. 3. Combine the carrots with the remaining ingredients. 4. Mold 1 tablespoon of the mixture into a ball and press it down with your hand or a spoon to flatten it. Repeat until the rest of the mixture is used up. 5. Spritz the balls with cooking spray. 6. Arrange in the air fryer basket, taking care not to overlap any balls. Bake for 8 to 11 minutes, or until they're firm. 7. Serve warm.

Bacon Pinwheels

Prep time: 10 minutes | Cook time: 10 minutes | Makes 8 pinwheels

- 1 sheet puff pastry
- 2 tablespoons maple syrup
- 48 g brown sugar
- 8 slices bacon
- Ground black pepper, to taste
- Cooking spray

1. Preheat the air fryer to 180°C. 2. Spritz the air fryer basket with cooking spray. 3. Roll the puff pastry into a 10-inch square with a rolling pin on a clean work surface, then cut the pastry into 8 strips. 4. Brush the strips with maple syrup and sprinkle with sugar, leaving a 1-inch far end uncovered. 5. Arrange each slice of bacon on each strip, leaving a ⅛-inch length of bacon hang over the end close to you. Sprinkle with black pepper. 6. From the end close to you, roll the strips into pinwheels, then dab the uncovered end with water and seal the rolls. 7. Arrange the pinwheels in the preheated air fryer and spritz with cooking spray. 8. Air fry for 10 minutes or until golden brown. 9. Flip the pinwheels halfway through. 10. Serve immediately.

CHAPTER 3 Treats and Desserts

Butter Flax Cookies

Prep time: 25 minutes | Cook time: 20 minutes |
Serves 4

- 115 g ground almonds
- 2 tablespoons flaxseed meal
- 30 g monk fruit, or equivalent sweetener
- 1 teaspoon baking powder
- A pinch of grated nutmeg
- A pinch of coarse salt
- 1 large egg, room temperature.
- 110 g unsalted butter, room temperature
- 1 teaspoon vanilla extract

1. Mix the ground almonds, flaxseed meal, monk fruit, baking powder, grated nutmeg, and salt in a bowl. 2. In a separate bowl, whisk the egg, butter, and vanilla extract. 3. Stir the egg mixture into dry mixture; mix to combine well or until it forms a nice, soft dough. 4. Roll your dough out and cut out with a biscuit cutter of your choice. Bake in the preheated air fryer at 180ºC for 10 minutes. Decrease the temperature to 160ºC and cook for 10 minutes longer. Bon appétit!

Carrot Cake with Cream Cheese Icing

Prep time: 10 minutes | Cook time: 55 minutes | Serves
6 to 8

- 80 g Plain flour
- 1 teaspoon baking powder
- ½ teaspoon baking soda
- 1 teaspoon ground cinnamon
- ¼ teaspoon ground nutmeg
- ¼ teaspoon salt
- 3 to 4 medium carrots or 2 large, grated
- 120 g granulated sugar
- 35 g brown sugar
- 2 eggs
- 175 ml canola or vegetable oil
- Icing:
- 225 g cream cheese, softened at room temperature
- 8 tablespoons butter, softened at room temperature

- 70 g icing sugar
- 1 teaspoon pure vanilla extract

1. Grease a cake pan. 2. Combine the flour, baking powder, baking soda, cinnamon, nutmeg, and salt in a bowl. Add the grated carrots and toss well. In a separate bowl, beat the sugars and eggs together until light and frothy. Drizzle in the oil, beating constantly. Fold the egg mixture into the dry ingredients until everything is just combined and you no longer see any traces of flour. Pour the batter into the cake pan and wrap the pan completely in greased aluminium foil. 3. Preheat the air fryer to 180ºC. 4. Lower the cake pan into the air fryer basket using a sling made of aluminium foil (fold a piece of aluminium foil into a strip about 2-inches wide by 24-inches long). Fold the ends of the aluminium foil into the air fryer, letting them rest on top of the cake. Air fry for 40 minutes. Remove the aluminium foil cover and air fry for an additional 15 minutes or until a skewer inserted into the center of the cake comes out clean and the top is nicely browned. 5. While the cake is cooking, beat the cream cheese, butter, icing sugar and vanilla extract together using a hand mixer, stand mixer or food processor (or a lot of elbow grease!). 6. Remove the cake pan from the air fryer and let the cake cool in the cake pan for 10 minutes or so. Then remove the cake from the pan and let it continue to cool completely. Frost the cake with the cream cheese icing and serve.

Classic Churros

Prep time: 35 minutes | Cook time: 10 minutes per
batch | Makes 12 churros

- 4 tablespoons butter
- ¼ teaspoon salt
- 120 ml water
- 60 g plain flour
- 2 large eggs
- 2 teaspoons ground cinnamon
- 35 g granulated white sugar
- Cooking spray

1. Put the butter, salt, and water in a saucepan 2.Bring to a boil until the butter is melted on high heat 3.Keep stirring 4.Reduce the heat to medium and fold in the flour to form a dough

5.Keep cooking and stirring until the dough is dried out and coat the pan with a crust 6.Turn off the heat and scrape the dough in a large bowl 7.Allow to cool for 15 minutes 8.Break and whisk the eggs into the dough with a hand mixer until the dough is sanity and firm enough to shape 9.Scoop up 1 tablespoon of the dough and roll it into a ½-inch-diameter and 2-inch-long cylinder 10.Repeat with remaining dough to make 12 cylinders in total 11.Combine the cinnamon and sugar in a large bowl and dunk the cylinders into the cinnamon mix to coat 12.Arrange the cylinders on a plate and refrigerate for 20 minutes 13.Preheat the air fryer to 190ºC 14.Spritz the air fryer basket with cooking spray 15.Place the cylinders in batches in the air fryer basket and spritz with cooking spray 16.Air fry for 10 minutes or until golden brown and fluffy 17.Flip them halfway through 18.Serve immediately.

Crispy Pineapple Rings

Prep time: 5 minutes | Cook time: 6 to 8 minutes | Serves 6

- ◆ 240 ml rice milk
- ◆ 45 g Plain flour
- ◆ 120 ml water
- ◆ 25 g unsweetened flaked coconut
- ◆ 4 tablespoons granulated sugar
- ◆ ½ teaspoon baking soda
- ◆ ½ teaspoon baking powder
- ◆ ½ teaspoon vanilla essence
- ◆ ½ teaspoon ground cinnamon
- ◆ ¼ teaspoon ground star anise
- ◆ Pinch of kosher, or coarse sea salt
- ◆ 1 medium pineapple, peeled and sliced

1. Preheat the air fryer to 190ºC. 2. In a large bowl, stir together all the ingredients except the pineapple. 3. Dip each pineapple slice into the batter until evenly coated. 4. Arrange the pineapple slices in the basket and air fry for 6 to 8 minutes until golden brown. 5. Remove from the basket to a plate and cool for 5 minutes before serving warm.

Baked Apples and Walnuts

Prep time: 6 minutes | Cook time: 20 minutes | Serves 4

- ◆ 4 small Granny Smith apples
- ◆ 50 g chopped walnuts
- ◆ 40 g light brown sugar

- ◆ 2 tablespoons butter, melted
- ◆ 1 teaspoon ground cinnamon
- ◆ ½ teaspoon ground nutmeg
- ◆ 120 ml water, or apple juice

1. Cut off the top third of the apples. Spoon out the core and some of the flesh and discard. Place the apples in a small air fryer baking pan. 2. Insert the crisper plate into the basket and the basket into the unit. Preheat to 180ºC. 3. In a small bowl, stir together the walnuts, brown sugar, melted butter, cinnamon, and nutmeg. Spoon this mixture into the centers of the hollowed-out apples. 4. Once the unit is preheated, pour the water into the crisper plate. Place the baking pan into the basket. 5. Bake for 20 minutes. 6. When the cooking is complete, the apples should be bubbly and fork tender.

Applesauce and Chocolate Brownies

Prep time: 10 minutes | Cook time: 15 minutes | Serves 8

- ◆ 15 g unsweetened cocoa powder
- ◆ 15 g Plain flour
- ◆ ¼ teaspoon kosher, or coarse sea salt
- ◆ ½ teaspoons baking powder
- ◆ 3 tablespoons unsalted butter, melted
- ◆ 80 g granulated sugar
- ◆ 1 large egg
- ◆ 3 tablespoons unsweetened apple sauce
- ◆ 50 g miniature semisweet chocolate crisps
- ◆ Coarse sea salt, to taste

1. Preheat the air fryer to 150ºC. 2. In a large bowl, whisk together the cocoa powder, Plain flour, kosher salt, and baking powder. 3. In a separate large bowl, combine the butter, granulated sugar, egg, and apple sauce, then use a spatula to fold in the cocoa powder mixture and the chocolate crisps until well combined. 4. Spray a baking pan with nonstick cooking spray, then pour the mixture into the pan. Place the pan in the air fryer and bake for 15 minutes or until a toothpick comes out clean when inserted in the middle. 5. Remove the brownies from the air fryer, sprinkle some coarse sea salt on top, and allow to cool in the pan on a wire rack for 20 minutes before cutting and serving.

Chocolate Soufflés

Prep time: 5 minutes | Cook time: 14 minutes | Serves

- Butter and sugar for greasing the ramekins
- 85 g semi-sweet chocolate, chopped
- 55 g unsalted butter
- 2 eggs, yolks and white separated
- 3 tablespoons granulated sugar
- ½ teaspoon pure vanilla extract
- 2 tablespoons Plain flour
- Icing sugar, for dusting the finished soufflés
- Heavy cream, for serving

1. Butter and sugar two 6-ounce (170 g) ramekins. (Butter the ramekins and then coat the butter with sugar by shaking it around in the ramekin and dumping out any excess.) 2. Melt the chocolate and butter together, either in the microwave or in a double boiler. In a separate bowl, beat the egg yolks vigorously. Add the sugar and the vanilla extract and beat well again. Drizzle in the chocolate and butter, mixing well. Stir in the flour, combining until there are no lumps. 3. Preheat the air fryer to 160ºC. 4. In a separate bowl, whisk the egg whites to soft peak stage (the point at which the whites tin almost stand up on the end of your whisk). Fold the whipped egg whites into the chocolate mixture gently and in stages. 5. Transfer the batter carefully to the buttered ramekins, leaving about ½-inch at the top. (You may have a little extra batter, depending on how airy the batter is, so you might be able to squeeze out a third soufflé if you want to.) Place the ramekins into the air fryer basket and air fry for 14 minutes. The soufflés should have risen nicely and be brown on top. (Don't worry if the top gets a little dark, you'll be covering it with icing sugar in the next step.) 6. Dust with icing sugar and serve immediately with double cream to pour over the top at the table.

Roasted Honey Pears

Prep time: 7 minutes | Cook time: 18 to 23 minutes |
Serves 4

- 2 large Bosc pears, halved lengthwise and seeded
- 3 tablespoons honey
- 1 tablespoon unsalted butter

- ½ teaspoon ground cinnamon
- 30 g walnuts, chopped
- 55 g part-skim ricotta cheese, divided

1. Insert the crisper plate into the basket and the basket into the unit. Preheat to 180ºC. 2. In a 6-by-2-inch round pan, place the pears cut-side up. 3. In a small microwave-safe bowl, melt the honey, butter, and cinnamon. Brush this mixture over the cut sides of the pears. Pour 3 tablespoons of water around the pears in the pan. 4. Once the unit is preheated, place the pan into the basket. 5. After about 18 minutes, check the pears. They should be tender when pierced with a fork and slightly crisp on the edges. If not, resume cooking. 6. When the cooking is complete, baste the pears once with the liquid in the pan. Carefully remove the pears from the pan and place on a serving plate. Drizzle each with some liquid from the pan, sprinkle the walnuts on top, and serve with a spoonful of ricotta cheese.

Chocolate Bread Pudding

Prep time: 10 minutes | Cook time: 10 to 12 minutes |
Serves 4

- Nonstick, flour-infused baking spray
- 1 egg
- 1 egg yolk
- 175 ml chocolate milk
- 2 tablespoons cocoa powder
- 3 tablespoons light brown sugar
- 3 tablespoons peanut butter
- 1 teaspoon vanilla extract
- 5 slices firm white bread, cubed

1. Spray a 6-by-2-inch round baking pan with the baking spray. Set aside. 2. In a medium bowl, whisk the egg, egg yolk, chocolate milk, cocoa powder, brown sugar, peanut butter, and vanilla until thoroughly combined. Stir in the bread cubes and let soak for 10 minutes. Spoon this mixture into the prepared pan. 3. Insert the crisper plate into the basket and the basket into the unit. Preheat the unit to 160ºC. 4. cook the pudding for about 10 minutes and then check if done. It is done when it is firm to the touch. If not, resume cooking. 5. When the cooking is complete, let the pudding cool for 5 minutes. Serve warm.

CHAPTER 4 Fish and Seafood

Cajun Salmon

Prep time: 5 minutes | Cook time: 7 minutes | Serves 2

- ◆ 2 salmon fillets, skin removed, 100 g each
- ◆ 2 tablespoons unsalted butter, melted
- ◆ ⅛ teaspoon ground cayenne pepper
- ◆ ½ teaspoon garlic powder
- ◆ 1 teaspoon paprika
- ◆ ¼ teaspoon ground black pepper

1. Brush each fillet with butter. 2. Combine remaining ingredients in a small bowl and then rub onto fish. Place fillets into the air fryer basket. 3. Adjust the temperature to 200ºC and air fry for 7 minutes. 4. When fully cooked, internal temperature will be 64ºC. Serve immediately.

Coconut Prawns with Spicy Dipping Sauce

Prep time: 15 minutes | Cook time: 8 minutes | Serves 4

- ◆ 70 g pork scratchings
- ◆ 70 g desiccated, unsweetened coconut
- ◆ 45 g coconut flour
- ◆ 1 teaspoon onion powder
- ◆ 1 teaspoon garlic powder
- ◆ 2 eggs
- ◆ 680 g large prawns, peeled and deveined
- ◆ ½ teaspoon salt
- ◆ ¼ teaspoon freshly ground black pepper
- ◆ Spicy Dipping Sauce:
- ◆ 115 g mayonnaise
- ◆ 2 tablespoons Sriracha
- ◆ Zest and juice of ½ lime
- ◆ 1 clove garlic, minced

1. Preheat the air fryer to 200ºC. 2. In a food processor fitted with a metal blade, combine the pork scratchings and desiccated coconut. Pulse until the mixture resembles coarse crumbs. Transfer to a shallow bowl. 3. In another shallow bowl, combine the coconut flour, onion powder, and garlic powder; mix until thoroughly combined. 4. In a third shallow bowl, whisk the eggs until slightly frothy. 5. In a large bowl, season the prawns with the salt and pepper, tossing gently to coat. 6. Working a few pieces at a time, dredge the prawns in the flour mixture, followed by the eggs, and finishing with the pork rind crumb mixture. Arrange the prawns on a baking sheet until ready to air fry. 7. Working in batches if necessary, arrange the prawns in a single layer in the air fryer basket. Pausing halfway through the cooking time to turn the prawns, air fry for 8 minutes until cooked through. 8. To make the sauce: In a small bowl, combine the mayonnaise, Sriracha, lime zest and juice, and garlic. Whisk until thoroughly combined. Serve alongside the prawns.

Trout Amandine with Lemon Butter Sauce

Prep time: 20 minutes | Cook time:8 minutes | Serves 4

Trout Amandine:

65 g toasted almonds

30 g grated Parmesan cheese

1 teaspoon salt

½ teaspoon freshly ground black pepper

2 tablespoons butter, melted

4 trout fillets, or salmon fillets, 110 g each

Cooking spray

Lemon Butter Sauce:

8 tablespoons butter, melted

2 tablespoons freshly squeezed lemon juice

½ teaspoon Worcestershire sauce

½ teaspoon salt

½ teaspoon freshly ground black pepper

¼ teaspoon hot sauce

1. In a blender or food processor, pulse the almonds for 5 to 10 seconds until finely processed. Transfer to a shallow bowl and whisk in the Parmesan cheese, salt, and pepper. Place the melted butter in another shallow bowl. 2. One at a time, dip the fish in the melted butter, then the almond mixture, coating thoroughly. 3. Preheat the air fryer to 150ºC. Line the air fryer basket with baking paper. 4. Place the coated fish on the baking paper and spritz with oil. 5. Bake for 4 minutes. Flip the fish, spritz it with oil, and bake for 4 minutes more until the fish

flakes easily with a fork. 6. In a small bowl, whisk the butter, lemon juice, Worcestershire sauce, salt, pepper, and hot sauce until blended. 7. Serve with the fish.

Salmon Fritters with Courgette

Prep time: 15 minutes | Cook time: 12 minutes | Serves 4

- ◆ 2 tablespoons almond flour
- ◆ 1 courgette, grated
- ◆ 1 egg, beaten
- ◆ 170 g salmon fillet, diced
- ◆ 1 teaspoon avocado oil
- ◆ ½ teaspoon ground black pepper

1. Mix almond flour with courgette, egg, salmon, and ground black pepper. 2. Then make the fritters from the salmon mixture. 3. Sprinkle the air fryer basket with avocado oil and put the fritters inside. 4. Cook the fritters at 190°C for 6 minutes per side.

Pesto Prawns with Wild Rice Pilaf

Prep time: 5 minutes | Cook time: 5 minutes | Serves 4

- ◆ 455 g medium prawns, peeled and deveined
- ◆ 60 g pesto sauce
- ◆ 1 lemon, sliced
- ◆ 390 g cooked wild rice pilaf

1. Preheat the air fryer to 180°C. 2. In a medium bowl, toss the prawns with the pesto sauce until well coated. 3. Place the prawns in a single layer in the air fryer basket. Put the lemon slices over the prawns and roast for 5 minutes. 4. Remove the lemons and discard. Serve a quarter of the prawns over 100 g wild rice with some favourite steamed vegetables.

Pecan-Crusted Tilapia

Prep time: 10minutes | Cook time: 10 minutes | Serves 4

160 g pecans

25 g panko bread crumbs

35 g plain flour

2 tablespoons Cajun seasoning

2 eggs, beaten with 2 tablespoons water

4 tilapia fillets, 170g each

Vegetable oil, for spraying

Lemon wedges, for serving

1. Grind the pecans in the food processor until they resemble coarse meal. Combine the ground pecans with the panko on a plate. On a second plate, combine the flour and Cajun seasoning. Dry the tilapia fillets using paper towels and dredge them in the flour mixture, shaking off any excess. Dip the fillets in the egg mixture and then dredge them in the pecan and panko mixture, pressing the coating onto the fillets. Place the breaded fillets on a plate or rack. 2. Preheat the air fryer to 190°C. Spray both sides of the breaded fillets with oil. Carefully transfer 2 of the fillets to the air fryer basket and air fry for 9 to 10 minutes, flipping once halfway through, until the flesh is opaque and flaky. Repeat with the remaining fillets. 3. Serve immediately with lemon wedges.

Sole and Asparagus Bundles

Prep time: 10 minutes | Cook time: 14 minutes | Serves 2

- ◆ 230 g asparagus, trimmed
- ◆ 1 teaspoon extra-virgin olive oil, divided
- ◆ Salt and pepper, to taste
- ◆ 4 (85 g) skinless sole fillets, ⅛ to ¼ inch thick
- ◆ 4 tablespoons unsalted butter, softened
- ◆ 1 small shallot, minced
- ◆ 1 tablespoon chopped fresh tarragon
- ◆ ¼ teaspoon lemon zest plus ½ teaspoon juice
- ◆ Vegetable oil spray

1. Preheat the air fryer to 150°C. 2. Toss asparagus with ½ teaspoon oil, pinch salt, and pinch pepper in a bowl. Cover and microwave until bright green and just tender, about 3 minutes, tossing halfway through microwaving. Uncover and set aside to cool slightly. 3. Make foil sling for air fryer basket by folding 1 long sheet of aluminium foil so it is 4 inches wide. Lay sheet of foil widthwise across basket, pressing foil into and up sides of basket. Fold excess foil as needed so that edges of foil are flush with top of basket. Lightly spray foil and basket with vegetable oil spray. 4. Pat sole dry with paper towels and season with salt and pepper. Arrange fillets skinned side up on cutting board, with thicker ends closest to you. Arrange asparagus evenly across base of each fillet, then tightly roll fillets away from you around asparagus to form tidy bundles. 5. Rub bundles evenly with remaining ½ teaspoon oil and arrange seam side down on sling in prepared basket. Bake until asparagus is tender and sole flakes apart when gently prodded with a paring knife, 14 to 18 minutes, using a sling to rotate bundles halfway through cooking. 6. Combine butter, shallot, tarragon, and lemon zest and juice in a bowl. Using sling, carefully remove sole bundles

from air fryer and transfer to individual plates. Top evenly with butter mixture and serve.

Prawn and Cherry Tomato Kebabs

Prep time: 15 minutes | Cook time: 5 minutes | Serves 4

- 680 g jumbo prawns, cleaned, peeled and deveined
- 455 g cherry tomatoes
- 2 tablespoons butter, melted
- 1 tablespoons Sriracha sauce
- Sea salt and ground black pepper, to taste
- 1 teaspoon dried parsley flakes
- ½ teaspoon dried basil
- ½ teaspoon dried oregano
- ½ teaspoon mustard seeds
- ½ teaspoon marjoram
- Special Equipment:
- 4 to 6 wooden skewers, soaked in water for 30 minutes

1. Preheat the air fryer to 200°C. 2. Put all the ingredients in a large bowl and toss to coat well. 3. Make the kebabs: Thread, alternating jumbo prawns and cherry tomatoes, onto the wooden skewers that fit into the air fryer. 4. Arrange the kebabs in the air fryer basket. You may need to cook in batches depending on the size of your air fryer basket. 5. Air fry for 5 minutes, or until the prawns are pink and the cherry tomatoes are softened. Repeat with the remaining kebabs. Let the prawns and cherry tomato kebabs cool for 5 minutes and serve hot.

Italian Tuna Roast

Prep time: 15 minutes | Cook time: 21 to 24 minutes | Serves 8

- Cooking spray
- 1 tablespoon Italian seasoning
- ⅛ teaspoon ground black pepper
- 1 tablespoon extra-light olive oil
- 1 teaspoon lemon juice
- 1 (900 g) tuna loin, 3 to 4 inches thick

1. Spray baking dish with cooking spray and place in air fryer basket. Preheat the air fryer to 200°C. 2. Mix together the Italian seasoning, pepper, oil, and lemon juice. 3. Using a dull table knife or butter knife, pierce top of tuna about every half inch: Insert knife into top of tuna roast and pierce almost all the way to the bottom. 4. Spoon oil mixture into each of the holes and use the knife to push seasonings into the tuna as deeply as possible. 5. Spread any remaining oil mixture on all outer surfaces of tuna. 6. Place tuna roast in baking dish and roast for 20 minutes. Check temperature with a meat thermometer. Cook for an additional 1 to 4 minutes or until temperature reaches 64°C. 7. Remove basket from the air fryer and let tuna sit in the basket for 10 minutes.

Tuna and Fruit Kebabs

Prep time: 15 minutes | Cook time: 8 to 12 minutes | Serves 4

- 455 g tuna steaks, cut into 1-inch cubes
- 85 g canned pineapple chunks, drained, juice reserved
- 75 g large red grapes
- 1 tablespoon honey
- 2 teaspoons grated fresh ginger
- 1 teaspoon olive oil
- Pinch cayenne pepper

1. Thread the tuna, pineapple, and grapes on 8 bamboo or 4 metal skewers that fit in the air fryer. 2. In a small bowl, whisk the honey, 1 tablespoon of reserved pineapple juice, the ginger, olive oil, and cayenne. Brush this mixture over the kebabs. Let them stand for 10 minutes. 3. Air fry the kebabs at 190°C for 8 to 12 minutes, or until the tuna reaches an internal temperature of at least 64°C on a meat thermometer, and the fruit is tender and glazed, brushing once with the remaining sauce. Discard any remaining marinade. Serve immediately.

Prawn Creole Casserole

Prep time: 20 minutes | Cook time: 25 minutes | Serves 4

- 360 g prawns, peeled and deveined
- 50 g chopped celery
- 50 g chopped onion
- 50 g chopped green pepper
- 2 large eggs, beaten
- 240 ml single cream
- 1 tablespoon butter, melted
- 1 tablespoon cornflour
- 1 teaspoon Creole seasoning
- ¾ teaspoon salt
- ½ teaspoon freshly ground black pepper

- 120 g shredded Cheddar cheese
- Cooking spray

1. In a medium bowl, stir together the prawns, celery, onion, and green pepper. 2. In another medium bowl, whisk the eggs, single cream, butter, cornflour, Creole seasoning, salt, and pepper until blended. Stir the egg mixture into the prawn mixture. Add the cheese and stir to combine. 3. Preheat the air fryer to 150°C. Spritz a baking pan with oil. 4. Transfer the prawn mixture to the prepared pan and place it in the air fryer basket. 5. Bake for 25 minutes, stirring every 10 minutes, until a knife inserted into the center comes out clean. 6. Serve immediately.

Chilli Prawns

Prep time: 10 minutes | Cook time: 8 minutes | Serves 2

- 8 prawns, peeled and deveined
- Salt and black pepper, to taste
- ½ teaspoon ground cayenne pepper
- ½ teaspoon garlic powder
- ½ teaspoon ground cumin
- ½ teaspoon red chilli flakes
- Cooking spray

1. Preheat the air fryer to 170°C. Spritz the air fryer basket with cooking spray. 2. Toss the remaining ingredients in a large bowl until the prawns are well coated. 3. Spread the coated prawns evenly in the basket and spray them with cooking spray. 4. Air fry for 8 minutes, flipping the prawns halfway through, or until the prawns are pink. 5. Remove the prawns from the basket to a plate.

Pecan-Crusted Catfish

Prep time: 5 minutes | Cook time: 12 minutes | Serves 4

- 65 g pecans, finely crushed
- 1 teaspoon fine sea salt
- ¼ teaspoon ground black pepper
- 4 catfish fillets, 110g each
- For Garnish (Optional):
- Fresh oregano
- Pecan halves

1. Spray the air fryer basket with avocado oil. Preheat the air fryer to 190°C. 2. In a large bowl, mix the crushed pecan, salt, and pepper. One at a time, dredge the catfish fillets in the mixture, coating them well. Use your hands to press the pecan meal into the fillets. Spray the fish with avocado oil and place them in the air fryer basket. 3. Air fry the coated catfish for 12 minutes, or until it flakes easily and is no longer translucent in the center, flipping halfway through. 4. Garnish with oregano sprigs and pecan halves, if desired. 5. Store leftovers in an airtight container in the fridge for up to 3 days. Reheat in a preheated 180°C air fryer for 4 minutes, or until heated through.

Crispy Prawns with Coriander

Prep time: 40 minutes | Cook time: 10 minutes | Serves 4

- 455 g raw large prawns, peeled and deveined with tails on or off
- 30 g chopped fresh coriander
- Juice of 1 lime
- 35 g plain flour
- 1 egg
- 40 g bread crumbs
- Salt and freshly ground black pepper, to taste
- Cooking oil spray
- 240 ml seafood sauce

1. Place the prawns in a resealable plastic bag and add the coriander and lime juice. Seal the bag. Shake it to combine. Marinate the prawns in the refrigerator for 30 minutes. 2. Place the flour in a small bowl. 3. In another small bowl, beat the egg. 4. Place the bread crumbs in a third small bowl, season with salt and pepper, and stir to combine. 5. Insert the crisper plate into the basket and the basket into the unit. Preheat the unit to 200°C.6. Remove the prawns from the plastic bag. Dip each in the flour, the egg, and the bread crumbs to coat. Gently press the crumbs onto the prawns. 7. Once the unit is preheated, spray the crisper plate and the basket with cooking oil. Place the prawns in the basket. It is okay to stack them. Spray the prawns with the cooking oil. 8. Cook for 4 minutes, remove the basket and flip the prawns one at a time. Reinsert the basket to resume cooking. 10. When the cooking is complete, the prawns should be crisp. Let cool for 5 minutes. Serve with cocktail sauce.

Prawn Dejonghe Skewers

Prep time: 10 minutes | Cook time: 15 minutes | Serves 4

- 2 teaspoons sherry, or apple cider vinegar
- 3 tablespoons unsalted butter, melted
- 60 g panko bread crumbs
- 3 cloves garlic, minced
- 8 g minced flat-leaf parsley, plus more for garnish
- 1 teaspoon kosher salt
- Pinch of cayenne pepper
- 680 g prawns, peeled and deveined
- Vegetable oil, for spraying
- Lemon wedges, for serving

1. Stir the sherry and melted butter together in a shallow bowl or pie plate and whisk until combined. Set aside. Whisk together the panko, garlic, parsley, salt, and cayenne pepper on a large plate or shallow bowl. 2. Thread the prawns onto metal skewers designed for the air fryer or bamboo skewers, 3 to 4 per skewer. Dip 1 prawns skewer in the butter mixture, then dredge in the panko mixture until each prawns is lightly coated. Place the skewer on a plate or rimmed baking sheet and repeat the process with the remaining skewers. 3. Preheat the air fryer to 180ºC. Arrange 4 skewers in the air fryer basket. Spray the skewers with oil and air fry for 8 minutes, until the bread crumbs are golden brown and the prawns are cooked through. Transfer the cooked skewers to a serving plate and keep warm while cooking the remaining 4 skewers in the air fryer. 4. Sprinkle the cooked skewers with additional fresh parsley and serve with lemon wedges if desired.

Tuna Steaks with Olive Tapenade

Prep time: 10 minutes | Cook time: 10 minutes | Serves 4

- 4 (170 g) ahi tuna steaks
- 1 tablespoon olive oil
- Salt and freshly ground black pepper, to taste
- ½ lemon, sliced into 4 wedges
- Olive Tapenade:
- 90 g pitted Kalamata olives
- 1 tablespoon olive oil
- 1 tablespoon chopped fresh parsley
- 1 clove garlic
- 2 teaspoons red wine vinegar
- 1 teaspoon capers, drained

1. Preheat the air fryer to 200ºC. 2. Drizzle the tuna steaks with the olive oil and sprinkle with salt and black pepper. Arrange the tuna steaks in a single layer in the air fryer basket. Pausing to turn the steaks halfway through the cooking time, air fry for 10 minutes until the fish is firm. 3. To make the tapenade: In a food processor fitted with a metal blade, combine the olives, olive oil, parsley, garlic, vinegar, and capers. Pulse until the mixture is finely chopped, pausing to scrape down the sides of the bowl if necessary. Spoon the tapenade over the top of the tuna steaks and serve with lemon wedges.

Garlic Prawns

Prep time: 15 minutes | Cook time: 10 minutes | Serves 3

- Prawns:
- Olive or vegetable oil, for spraying
- 450 g medium raw prawns, peeled and deveined
- 6 tablespoons unsalted butter, melted
- 60 g panko bread crumbs
- 2 tablespoons garlic granules
- 1 teaspoon salt
- ½ teaspoon freshly ground black pepper
- Garlic Butter Sauce:
- 115 g unsalted butter
- 2 teaspoons garlic granules
- ¾ teaspoon salt (omit if using salted butter)

Make the Prawns 1. Preheat the air fryer to 200ºC. Line the air fryer basket with baking paper and spray lightly with oil. 2. Place the prawns and melted butter in a zip-top plastic bag, seal, and shake well, until evenly coated. 3. In a medium bowl, mix together the breadcrumbs, garlic, salt, and black pepper. 4. Add the prawns to the panko mixture and toss until evenly coated. Shake off any excess coating. 5. Place the prawns in the prepared basket and spray lightly with oil. 6. Cook for 8 to 10 minutes, flipping and spraying with oil after 4 to 5 minutes, until golden brown and crispy. Make the Garlic Butter Sauce 7. In a microwave-safe bowl, combine the butter, garlic, and salt and microwave on 50% power for 30 to 60 seconds, stirring every 15 seconds, until completely melted. 8. Serve the prawns immediately with the garlic butter sauce on the side for dipping.

Crab Cakes with Mango Mayo

Prep time: 25 minutes | Cook time: 15 minutes | Serves 4

- Crab Cakes:
- 235 g chopped red onion

- 8 g fresh coriander leaves
- 1 small serrano chilli or jalapeño, seeded and quartered
- 230 g lump crab meat
- 1 large egg
- 1 tablespoon mayonnaise
- 1 tablespoon whole-grain mustard
- 2 teaspoons minced fresh ginger
- ½ teaspoon ground cumin
- ½ teaspoon ground coriander
- ¼ teaspoon kosher or coarse sea salt
- 2 tablespoons fresh lemon juice
- 45 g panko bread crumbs
- Vegetable oil spray
- Mango Mayo:
- 80 g diced fresh mango
- 115 g mayonnaise
- ½ teaspoon grated lime zest
- 2 teaspoons fresh lime juice
- Pinch of cayenne pepper

1. For the crab cakes: Combine the onion, coriander leaves, and serrano in a food processor. Pulse until minced. 2. In a large bowl, combine the minced vegetable mixture with the crab meat, egg, mayonnaise, mustard, ginger, cumin, ground coriander, and salt. Add the lemon juice and mix gently until thoroughly combined. Add 60 g of the bread crumbs. Mix gently again until well blended. 3. Form into four evenly sized patties. Put the remaining 30 g bread crumbs in a shallow bowl and press both sides of each patty into the bread crumbs. 4. Arrange the patties in the air fryer basket. Spray with vegetable oil spray. Set the air fryer to 190°C for 15 minutes, turning and spraying other side of the patties with vegetable oil spray halfway through the cooking time, until the crab cakes are golden brown and crisp. 5. Meanwhile, for the mayonnaise: In a blender, combine the mango, mayonnaise, lime zest, lime juice, and cayenne. Blend until smooth. 6. Serve the crab cakes warm, with the mango mayo.

Garlicky Cod Fillets

Prep time: 10 minutes | Cook time: 10 to 12 minutes | Serves 4

- 1 teaspoon olive oil
- 4 cod fillets
- ¼ teaspoon fine sea salt

- ¼ teaspoon ground black pepper, or more to taste
- 1 teaspoon cayenne pepper
- 8 g fresh Italian parsley, coarsely chopped
- 120 ml milk
- 1 Italian pepper, chopped
- 4 garlic cloves, minced
- 1 teaspoon dried basil
- ½ teaspoon dried oregano

1. Lightly coat the sides and bottom of a baking dish with the olive oil. Set aside. 2. In a large bowl, sprinkle the fillets with salt, black pepper, and cayenne pepper. 3. In a food processor, pulse the remaining ingredients until smoothly puréed. 4. Add the purée to the bowl of fillets and toss to coat, then transfer to the prepared baking dish. 5. Preheat the air fryer to 190°C. 6. Put the baking dish in the air fryer basket and bake for 10 to 12 minutes, or until the fish flakes when pressed lightly with a fork. 7. Remove from the basket and serve warm.

Cayenne Sole Cutlets

Prep time: 15 minutes | Cook time: 10 minutes | Serves 2

- 1 egg
- 120 g Pecorino Romano cheese, grated
- Sea salt and white pepper, to taste
- ½ teaspoon cayenne pepper
- 1 teaspoon dried parsley flakes
- 2 sole fillets

1. To make a breading station, whisk the egg until frothy. 2. In another bowl, mix Pecorino Romano cheese, and spices. 3. Dip the fish in the egg mixture and turn to coat evenly; then, dredge in the cracker crumb mixture, turning a couple of times to coat evenly. 4. Cook in the preheated air fryer at 200°C for 5 minutes; turn them over and cook another 5 minutes. Enjoy!

Almond-Crusted Fish

Prep time: 15 minutes | Cook time: 10 minutes | Serves 4

- 4 firm white fish fillets, 110g each
- 25 g breadcrumbs
- 20 g slivered almonds, crushed
- 2 tablespoons lemon juice
- ⅛ teaspoon cayenne
- Salt and pepper, to taste
- 470 g plain flour

- ◆ 1 egg, beaten with 1 tablespoon water
- ◆ Olive or vegetable oil for misting or cooking spray

1. Split fish fillets lengthwise down the center to create 8 pieces. 2. Mix breadcrumbs and almonds together and set aside. 3. Mix the lemon juice and cayenne together. Brush on all sides of fish. 4. Season fish to taste with salt and pepper. 5. Place the flour on a sheet of wax paper. 6. Roll fillets in flour, dip in egg wash, and roll in the crumb mixture. 7. Mist both sides of fish with oil or cooking spray. 8. Spray the air fryer basket and lay fillets inside. 9. Roast at 200ºC for 5 minutes, turn fish over, and cook for an additional 5 minutes or until fish is done and flakes easily.

Cajun and Lemon Pepper Cod

Prep time: 5 minutes | Cook time: 12 minutes | Makes 2 cod fillets

- ◆ 1 tablespoon Cajun seasoning
- ◆ 1 teaspoon salt
- ◆ ½ teaspoon lemon pepper
- ◆ ½ teaspoon freshly ground black pepper
- ◆ 2 cod fillets, 230 g each, cut to fit into the air fryer basket
- ◆ Cooking spray
- ◆ 2 tablespoons unsalted butter, melted
- ◆ 1 lemon, cut into 4 wedges

1. Preheat the air fryer to 180ºC. Spritz the air fryer basket with cooking spray. 2. Thoroughly combine the Cajun seasoning, salt, lemon pepper, and black pepper in a small bowl. Rub this mixture all over the cod fillets until completely coated. 3. Put the fillets in the air fryer basket and brush the melted butter over both sides of each fillet. 4. Bake in the preheated air fryer for 12 minutes, flipping the fillets halfway through, or until the fish flakes easily with a fork. 5. Remove the fillets from the basket and serve with fresh lemon wedges.

Savoury Prawns

Prep time: 5 minutes | Cook time: 8 to 10 minutes | Serves 4

- ◆ 455 g fresh large prawns, peeled and deveined
- ◆ 1 tablespoon avocado oil
- ◆ 2 teaspoons minced garlic, divided
- ◆ ½ teaspoon red pepper flakes
- ◆ Sea salt and freshly ground black pepper, to taste
- ◆ 2 tablespoons unsalted butter, melted
- ◆ 2 tablespoons chopped fresh parsley

1. Place the prawns in a large bowl and toss with the avocado oil, 1 teaspoon of minced garlic, and red pepper flakes. Season with salt and pepper. 2. Set the air fryer to 180ºC. Arrange the prawns in a single layer in the air fryer basket, working in batches if necessary. Cook for 6 minutes. Flip the prawns and cook for 2 to 4 minutes more, until the internal temperature of the prawns reaches 50ºC. (The time it takes to cook will depend on the size of the prawns.) 3. While the prawns are cooking, melt the butter in a small saucepan over medium heat and stir in the remaining 1 teaspoon of garlic. 4. Transfer the cooked prawns to a large bowl, add the garlic butter, and toss well. Top with the parsley and serve warm.

Creamy Haddock

Prep time: 10 minutes | Cook time: 8 minutes | Serves 4

- ◆ 455 g haddock fillet
- ◆ 1 teaspoon cayenne pepper
- ◆ 1 teaspoon salt
- ◆ 1 teaspoon coconut oil
- ◆ 120 ml double cream

1. Grease a baking pan with coconut oil. 2. Then put haddock fillet inside and sprinkle it with cayenne pepper, salt, and double cream. Put the baking pan in the air fryer basket and cook at 190ºC for 8 minutes.

Coconut Prawns

Prep time: 5 minutes | Cook time: 6 minutes | Serves 2

- ◆ 230 g medium prawns, peeled and deveined
- ◆ 2 tablespoons salted butter, melted
- ◆ ½ teaspoon Old Bay seasoning
- ◆ 25 g desiccated, unsweetened coconut

1. In a large bowl, toss the prawns in butter and Old Bay seasoning. 2. Place desiccated coconut in bowl. Coat each piece of prawns in the coconut and place into the air fryer basket. 3. Adjust the temperature to 200ºC and air fry for 6 minutes. 4. Gently turn the prawns halfway through the cooking time. Serve immediately.

Firecracker Prawns

Prep time: 10 minutes | Cook time: 7 minutes | Serves 4

- ◆ 455 g medium prawns, peeled and deveined
- ◆ 2 tablespoons salted butter, melted
- ◆ ½ teaspoon Old Bay seasoning

- ◆ ¼ teaspoon garlic powder
- ◆ 2 tablespoons Sriracha
- ◆ ¼ teaspoon powdered sweetener
- ◆ 60 ml full-fat mayonnaise
- ◆ ⅛ teaspoon ground black pepper

1. In a large bowl, toss prawns in butter, Old Bay seasoning, and garlic powder. Place prawns into the air fryer basket. 2. Adjust the temperature to 200ºC and set the timer for 7 minutes. 3. Flip the prawns halfway through the cooking time. Prawns will be bright pink when fully cooked. 4. In another large bowl, mix Sriracha, sweetener, mayonnaise, and pepper. Toss prawns in the spicy mixture and serve immediately.

Mackerel with Spinach

Prep time: 15 minutes | Cook time: 20 minutes | Serves 5

- ◆ 455 g mackerel, trimmed
- ◆ 1 pepper, chopped
- ◆ 15 g spinach, chopped
- ◆ 1 tablespoon avocado oil
- ◆ 1 teaspoon ground black pepper
- ◆ 1 teaspoon tomato paste

1. In the mixing bowl, mix pepper with spinach, ground black pepper, and tomato paste. 2. Fill the mackerel with spinach mixture. 3. Then brush the fish with avocado oil and put it in the air fryer. 4. Cook the fish at 190ºC for 20 minutes.

Golden Prawns

Prep time: 20 minutes | Cook time: 7 minutes | Serves 4

- ◆ 2 egg whites
- ◆ 30 g coconut flour
- ◆ 120 g Parmigiano-Reggiano, grated
- ◆ ½ teaspoon celery seeds

- ◆ ½ teaspoon porcini powder
- ◆ ½ teaspoon onion powder
- ◆ 1 teaspoon garlic powder
- ◆ ½ teaspoon dried rosemary
- ◆ ½ teaspoon sea salt
- ◆ ½ teaspoon ground black pepper
- ◆ 680 g prawns, peeled and deveined

1. Whisk the egg with coconut flour and Parmigiano-Reggiano. Add in seasonings and mix to combine well. 2. Dip your prawns in the batter. Roll until they are covered on all sides. 3. Cook in the preheated air fryer at 200ºC for 5 to 7 minutes or until golden brown. Work in batches. Serve with lemon wedges if desired.

Prawns with Smoky Tomato Dressing

Prep time: 5 minutes | Cook time: 8 minutes | Serves 2

- ◆ 3 tablespoons mayonnaise
- ◆ 1 tablespoon ketchup
- ◆ 1 tablespoon minced garlic
- ◆ 1 teaspoon Sriracha
- ◆ ½ teaspoon smoked paprika
- ◆ ½ teaspoon kosher or coarse sea salt
- ◆ 455 g large raw prawns (21 to 25 count), peeled (tails left on) and deveined
- ◆ Vegetable oil spray
- ◆ 50 g chopped spring onions

1. In a large bowl, combine the mayonnaise, ketchup, garlic, Sriracha, paprika, and salt. Add the prawns and toss to coat with the sauce. 2. Spray the air fryer basket with vegetable oil spray. Place the prawns in the basket. Set the air fryer to 180ºC for 8 minutes, tossing and spraying the prawns with vegetable oil spray halfway through the cooking time. 3. Sprinkle with the chopped spring onions before serving.

CHAPTER 5 Beef, Pork, and Lamb

Blue Cheese Steak Salad

Prep time: 30 minutes | Cook time: 22 minutes | Serves 4

- 2 tablespoons balsamic vinegar
- 2 tablespoons red wine vinegar
- 1 tablespoon Dijon mustard
- 1 tablespoon granulated sweetener
- 1 teaspoon minced garlic
- Sea salt and freshly ground black pepper, to taste
- 180 ml extra-virgin olive oil
- 450 g boneless rump steak
- Avocado oil spray
- 1 small red onion, cut into ¼-inch-thick rounds
- 170 g baby spinach
- 120 g cherry tomatoes, halved
- 85 g blue cheese, crumbled

1. In a blender, combine the balsamic vinegar, red wine vinegar, Dijon mustard, sweetener, and garlic. Season with salt and pepper and process until smooth. With the blender running, drizzle in the olive oil. Process until well combined. Transfer to a jar with a tight-fitting lid, and refrigerate until ready to serve (it will keep for up to 2 weeks). 2. Season the steak with salt and pepper and let sit at room temperature for at least 45 minutes, time permitting. 3. Set the air fryer to 200°C. Spray the steak with oil and place it in the air fryer basket. Air fry for 6 minutes. Flip the steak and spray it with more oil. Air fry for 6 minutes more for medium-rare or until the steak is done to your liking. 4. Transfer the steak to a plate, tent with a piece of aluminium foil, and allow it to rest. 5. Spray the onion slices with oil and place them in the air fryer basket. Cook at 200°C for 5 minutes. Flip the onion slices and spray them with more oil. Air fry for 5 minutes more. 6. Slice the steak diagonally into thin strips. Place the spinach, cherry tomatoes, onion slices, and steak in a large bowl. Toss with the desired amount of dressing. Sprinkle with crumbled blue cheese and serve.

Pork Loin with Aloha Salsa

Prep time: 20 minutes | Cook time: 7 to 9 minutes | Serves 4

- Aloha Salsa:
- 235 g fresh pineapple, chopped in small pieces
- 60 g red onion, finely chopped
- 60 g green or red pepper, chopped
- ½ teaspoon ground cinnamon
- 1 teaspoon reduced-salt soy sauce
- ⅛ teaspoon crushed red pepper
- ⅛ teaspoon ground black pepper
- 2 eggs
- 2 tablespoons milk
- 30 g flour
- 30 g panko bread crumbs
- 4 teaspoons sesame seeds
- 450 g boneless, thin pork loin or tenderloin (⅜ to ½-inch thick)
- Pepper and salt
- 30 g cornflour
- Oil for misting or cooking spray

1. In a medium bowl, stir together all ingredients for salsa. Cover and refrigerate while cooking pork. 2. Preheat the air fryer to 200°C. 3. Beat together eggs and milk in shallow dish. 4. In another shallow dish, mix together the flour, panko, and sesame seeds. 5. Sprinkle pork with pepper and salt to taste. 6. Dip pork in cornflour, egg mixture, and then panko coating. Spray both sides with oil or cooking spray. 7. Cook pork for 3 minutes. Turn pork over, spraying both sides, and continue cooking for 4 to 6 minutes or until well done. 8. Serve fried cutlets with salsa on the side.

Sweet and Spicy Country-Style Ribs

Prep time: 10 minutes | Cook time: 25 minutes | Serves 4

- 2 tablespoons brown sugar
- 2 tablespoons smoked paprika
- 1 teaspoon garlic powder
- 1 teaspoon onion granules
- 1 teaspoon mustard powder
- 1 teaspoon ground cumin
- 1 teaspoon coarse or flaky salt

- 1 teaspoon black pepper
- ¼ to ½ teaspoon cayenne pepper
- 680 g boneless pork steaks
- 235 ml barbecue sauce

1. In a small bowl, stir together the brown sugar, paprika, garlic powder, onion granules, mustard powder, cumin, salt, black pepper, and cayenne. Mix until well combined. 2. Pat the ribs dry with a paper towel. Generously sprinkle the rub evenly over both sides of the ribs and rub in with your fingers. 3. Place the ribs in the air fryer basket. Set the air fryer to 180°C for 15 minutes. Turn the ribs and brush with 120 ml of the barbecue sauce. Cook for an additional 10 minutes. Use a meat thermometer to ensure the pork has reached an internal temperature of 64°C. 4. Serve with remaining barbecue sauce.

Sirloin Steak with Honey-Mustard Butter

Prep time: 5 minutes | Cook time: 14 minutes | Serves 4

- 900 g beef sirloin steak
- 1 teaspoon cayenne pepper
- 1 tablespoon honey
- 1 tablespoon Dijon mustard
- ½ stick butter, softened
- Sea salt and freshly ground black pepper, to taste
- Cooking spray

1. Preheat the air fryer to 200°C and spritz with cooking spray. 2. Sprinkle the steak with cayenne pepper, salt, and black pepper on a clean work surface. 3. Arrange the steak in the preheated air fryer and spritz with cooking spray. 4. Air fry for 14 minutes or until browned and reach your desired doneness. Flip the steak halfway through. 5. Meanwhile, combine the honey, mustard, and butter in a small bowl. Stir to mix well. 6. Transfer the air fried steak onto a plate and baste with the honey-mustard butter before serving.

Banger-Stuffed Peppers

Prep time: 15 minutes | Cook time: 28 to 30 minutes | Serves 6

- Avocado oil spray
- 230 g Italian-seasoned banger, casings removed
- 120 g chopped mushrooms
- 60 g diced onion
- 1 teaspoon Italian seasoning

- Sea salt and freshly ground black pepper, to taste
- 235 ml keto-friendly marinara sauce
- 3 peppers, halved and seeded
- 85 g low-moisture Mozzarella or other melting cheese, shredded

1. Spray a large frying pan with oil and place it over medium-high heat. Add the banger and cook for 5 minutes, breaking up the meat with a wooden spoon. Add the mushrooms, onion, and Italian seasoning, and season with salt and pepper. Cook for 5 minutes more. Stir in the marinara sauce and cook until heated through. 2. Scoop the banger filling into the pepper halves. 3. Set the air fryer to 180°C. Arrange the peppers in a single layer in the air fryer basket, working in batches if necessary. Air fry for 15 minutes. 4. Top the stuffed peppers with the cheese and air fry for 3 to 5 minutes more, until the cheese is melted and the peppers are tender.

Lebanese Malfouf (Stuffed Cabbage Rolls)

Prep time: 15 minutes | Cook time: 33 minutes | Serves 4

- 1 head green cabbage
- 450 g lean beef mince
- 120 g long-grain brown rice
- 4 garlic cloves, minced
- 1 teaspoon salt
- ½ teaspoon black pepper
- 1 teaspoon ground cinnamon
- 2 tablespoons chopped fresh mint
- Juice of 1 lemon
- Olive oil cooking spray
- 120 ml beef stock
- 1 tablespoon olive oil

1. Cut the cabbage in half and remove the core. Remove 12 of the larger leaves to use for the cabbage rolls. 2. Bring a large pot of salted water to a boil, then drop the cabbage leaves into the water, boiling them for 3 minutes. Remove from the water and set aside. 3. In a large bowl, combine the beef, rice, garlic, salt, pepper, cinnamon, mint, and lemon juice, and mix together until combined. Divide this mixture into 12 equal portions. 4. Preheat the air fryer to 180°C. Lightly coat a small casserole dish with olive oil cooking spray. 5. Place a cabbage leaf on a clean work surface. Place a spoonful of the beef mixture on one side of the leaf, leaving space on all other sides. Fold the two

perpendicular sides inward and then roll forward, tucking tightly as rolled (similar to a burrito roll). Place the finished rolls into the baking dish, stacking them on top of each other if needed. 6. Pour the beef stock over the top of the cabbage rolls so that it soaks down between them, and then brush the tops with the olive oil. 7. Place the casserole dish into the air fryer basket and bake for 30 minutes.

Mediterranean Beef Steaks

Prep time: 20 minutes | Cook time: 20 minutes | Serves 4

- ◆ 2 tablespoons soy sauce or tamari
- ◆ 3 heaping tablespoons fresh chives
- ◆ 2 tablespoons olive oil
- ◆ 3 tablespoons dry white wine
- ◆ 4 small-sized beef steaks
- ◆ 2 teaspoons smoked cayenne pepper
- ◆ ½ teaspoon dried basil
- ◆ ½ teaspoon dried rosemary
- ◆ 1 teaspoon freshly ground black pepper
- ◆ 1 teaspoon sea salt, or more to taste

1. Firstly, coat the steaks with the cayenne pepper, black pepper, salt, basil, and rosemary. 2. Drizzle the steaks with olive oil, white wine, and soy sauce. 3. Finally, roast in the air fryer for 20 minutes at 170ºC. Serve garnished with fresh chives. Bon appétit!

Caraway Crusted Beef Steaks

Prep time: 5 minutes | Cook time: 10 minutes | Serves 4

- ◆ 4 beef steaks
- ◆ 2 teaspoons caraway seeds
- ◆ 2 teaspoons garlic powder
- ◆ Sea salt and cayenne pepper, to taste
- ◆ 1 tablespoon melted butter
- ◆ 40 g almond flour
- ◆ 2 eggs, beaten

1. Preheat the air fryer to 180ºC. 2. Add the beef steaks to a large bowl and toss with the caraway seeds, garlic powder, salt and pepper until well coated. 3. Stir together the melted butter and almond flour in a bowl. Whisk the eggs in a different bowl. 4. Dredge the seasoned steaks in the eggs, then dip in the almond and butter mixture. 5. Arrange the coated steaks in the air fryer basket. Air fryer for 10 minutes, or until the internal

temperature of the beef steaks reaches at least 64ºC on a meat thermometer. Flip the steaks once halfway through to ensure even cooking. 6. Transfer the steaks to plates. Let cool for 5 minutes and serve hot.

Cheddar Bacon Burst with Spinach

Prep time: 5 minutes | Cook time: 60 minutes | Serves 8

- ◆ 30 slices bacon
- ◆ 1 tablespoon Chipotle chilli powder
- ◆ 2 teaspoons Italian seasoning
- ◆ 120 g Cheddar cheese
- ◆ 1 kg raw spinach

1. Preheat the air fryer to 190ºC. 2. Weave the bacon into 15 vertical pieces and 12 horizontal pieces. Cut the extra 3 in half to fill in the rest, horizontally. 3. Season the bacon with Chipotle chilli powder and Italian seasoning. 4. Add the cheese to the bacon. 5. Add the spinach and press down to compress. 6. Tightly roll up the woven bacon. 7. Line a baking sheet with kitchen foil and add plenty of salt to it. 8. Put the bacon on top of a cooling rack and put that on top of the baking sheet. 9. Bake for 60 minutes. 10. Let cool for 15 minutes before slicing and serving.

Bacon and Cheese Stuffed Pork Chops

Prep time: 10 minutes | Cook time: 12 minutes | Serves 4

- ◆ 15 g plain pork scratchings, finely crushed
- ◆ 120 g shredded sharp Cheddar cheese
- ◆ 4 slices cooked bacon, crumbled
- ◆ 4 (110 g) boneless pork chops
- ◆ ½ teaspoon salt
- ◆ ¼ teaspoon ground black pepper

1. In a small bowl, mix pork scratchings, Cheddar, and bacon. 2. Make a 3-inch slit in the side of each pork chop and stuff with ¼ pork rind mixture. Sprinkle each side of pork chops with salt and pepper. 3. Place pork chops into ungreased air fryer basket, stuffed side up. Adjust the temperature to 200ºC and air fry for 12 minutes. Pork chops will be browned and have an internal temperature of at least 64ºC when done. Serve warm.

Greek Lamb Pitta Pockets

Prep time: 15 minutes | Cook time: 6 minutes | Serves

◆ Dressing:

◆ 235 ml plain yoghurt

◆ 1 tablespoon lemon juice

◆ 1 teaspoon dried dill, crushed

◆ 1 teaspoon ground oregano

◆ ½ teaspoon salt

◆ Meatballs:

◆ 230 g lamb mince

◆ 1 tablespoon diced onion

◆ 1 teaspoon dried parsley

◆ 1 teaspoon dried dill, crushed

◆ ¼ teaspoon oregano

◆ ¼ teaspoon coriander

◆ ¼ teaspoon ground cumin

◆ ¼ teaspoon salt

◆ 4 pitta halves

◆ Suggested Toppings:

◆ 1 red onion, slivered

◆ 1 medium cucumber, deseeded, thinly sliced

◆ Crumbled feta cheese

◆ Sliced black olives

◆ Chopped fresh peppers

1. Preheat the air fryer to 200°C. 2. Stir the dressing ingredients together in a small bowl and refrigerate while preparing lamb. 3. Combine all meatball ingredients in a large bowl and stir to distribute seasonings. 4. Shape meat mixture into 12 small meatballs, rounded or slightly flattened if you prefer. 5. Transfer the meatballs in the preheated air fryer and air fry for 6 minutes, until well done. Remove and drain on paper towels. 6. To serve, pile meatballs and the choice of toppings in pitta pockets and drizzle with dressing.

Currywurst

Prep time: 15 minutes | Cook time: 12 minutes | Serves 4

◆ 235 ml tomato sauce

◆ 2 tablespoons cider vinegar

◆ 2 teaspoons curry powder

◆ 2 teaspoons sweet paprika

◆ 1 teaspoon sugar

◆ ¼ teaspoon cayenne pepper

◆ 1 small onion, diced

◆ 450 g bratwurst, sliced diagonally into 1-inch pieces

1. In a large bowl, combine the tomato sauce, vinegar, curry powder, paprika, sugar, and cayenne. Whisk until well combined. Stir in the onion and bratwurst. 2. Transfer the mixture to a baking tray. Place the pan in the air fryer basket. Set the air fryer to 200°C for 12 minutes, or until the banger is heated through and the sauce is bubbling.

Fillet with Crispy Shallots

Prep time: 30 minutes | Cook time: 18 to 20 minutes | Serves 6

◆ 680 g beef fillet steaks

◆ Sea salt and freshly ground black pepper, to taste

◆ 4 medium shallots

◆ 1 teaspoon olive oil or avocado oil

1. Season both sides of the steaks with salt and pepper, and let them sit at room temperature for 45 minutes. 2. Set the air fryer to 200°C and let it preheat for 5 minutes. 3. Working in batches if necessary, place the steaks in the air fryer basket in a single layer and air fry for 5 minutes. Flip and cook for 5 minutes longer, until an instant-read thermometer inserted in the center of the steaks registers 49°C for medium-rare (or as desired). Remove the steaks and tent with aluminium foil to rest. 4. Set the air fryer to 150°C. In a medium bowl, toss the shallots with the oil. Place the shallots in the basket and air fry for 5 minutes, then give them a toss and cook for 3 to 5 minutes more, until crispy and golden brown. 5. Place the steaks on serving plates and arrange the shallots on top.

Bacon-Wrapped Vegetable Kebabs

Prep time: 10 minutes | Cook time: 10 to 12 minutes | Serves 4

◆ 110 g mushrooms, sliced

◆ 1 small courgette, sliced

◆ 12 baby plum tomatoes

◆ 110 g sliced bacon, halved

◆ Avocado oil spray

◆ Sea salt and freshly ground black pepper, to taste

1. Stack 3 mushroom slices, 1 courgette slice, and 1 tomato. Wrap a bacon strip around the vegetables and thread them onto a skewer. Repeat with the remaining vegetables and bacon. Spray with oil and sprinkle with salt and pepper. 2. Set the air fryer to 200°C. Place the skewers in the air fryer basket in a single layer, working in batches if necessary, and air fry for 5

minutes. Flip the skewers and cook for 5 to 7 minutes more, until the bacon is crispy and the vegetables are tender. 3. Serve warm.

Five-Spice Pork Belly

Prep time: 10 minutes | Cook time: 17 minutes | Serves 4

- 450 g unsalted pork belly
- 2 teaspoons Chinese five-spice powder
- Sauce:
- 1 tablespoon coconut oil
- 1 (1-inch) piece fresh ginger, peeled and grated
- 2 cloves garlic, minced
- 120 ml beef or chicken stock
- ¼ to 120 ml liquid or powdered sweetener
- 3 tablespoons wheat-free tamari
- 1 spring onion, sliced, plus more for garnish

1. Spray the air fryer basket with avocado oil. Preheat the air fryer to 200°C. 2. Cut the pork belly into ½-inch-thick slices and season well on all sides with the five-spice powder. Place the slices in a single layer in the air fryer basket (if you're using a smaller air fryer, work in batches if necessary) and cook for 8 minutes, or until cooked to your liking, flipping halfway through. 3. While the pork belly cooks, make the sauce: Heat the coconut oil in a small saucepan over medium heat. Add the ginger and garlic and sauté for 1 minute, or until fragrant. Add the stock, sweetener, and tamari and simmer for 10 to 15 minutes, until thickened. Add the spring onion and cook for another minute, until the spring onion is softened. Taste and adjust the seasoning to your liking. 4. Transfer the pork belly to a large bowl. Pour the sauce over the pork belly and coat well. Place the pork belly slices on a serving platter and garnish with sliced spring onions. 5. Best served fresh. Store leftovers in an airtight container in the fridge for up to 4 days. Reheat in a preheated 200°C air fryer for 3 minutes, or until heated through.

Pork Milanese

Prep time: 10 minutes | Cook time: 12 minutes | Serves 4

- 4 (1-inch) boneless pork chops
- Fine sea salt and ground black pepper, to taste
- 2 large eggs
- 180 g pre-grated Parmesan cheese

- Chopped fresh parsley, for garnish
- Lemon slices, for serving

1. Spray the air fryer basket with avocado oil. Preheat the air fryer to 200°C. 2. Place the pork chops between 2 sheets of cling film and pound them with the flat side of a meat tenderizer until they're ¼ inch thick. Lightly season both sides of the chops with salt and pepper. 3. Lightly beat the eggs in a shallow bowl. Divide the Parmesan cheese evenly between 2 bowls and set the bowls in this order: Parmesan, eggs, Parmesan. Dredge a chop in the first bowl of Parmesan, then dip it in the eggs, and then dredge it again in the second bowl of Parmesan, making sure both sides and all edges are well-coated. Repeat with the remaining chops. 4. Place the chops in the air fryer basket and air fry for 12 minutes, or until the internal temperature reaches 64°C, flipping halfway through. 5. Garnish with fresh parsley and serve immediately with lemon slices. Store leftovers in an airtight container in the refrigerator for up to 3 days. Reheat in a preheated 200°C air fryer for 5 minutes, or until warmed through.

Greek Stuffed Fillet

Prep time: 10 minutes | Cook time: 10 minutes | Serves 4

- 680 g venison or beef fillet, pounded to ¼ inch thick
- 3 teaspoons fine sea salt
- 1 teaspoon ground black pepper
- 60 g creamy goat cheese
- 120 g crumbled feta cheese (about 60 g)
- 60 g finely chopped onions
- 2 cloves garlic, minced
- For Garnish/Serving (Optional):
- Yellow/American mustard
- Halved cherry tomatoes
- Extra-virgin olive oil
- Sprigs of fresh rosemary
- Lavender flowers

1. Spray the air fryer basket with avocado oil. Preheat the air fryer to 200°C. 2. Season the fillet on all sides with the salt and pepper. 3. In a medium-sized mixing bowl, combine the goat cheese, feta, onions, and garlic. Place the mixture in the center of the tenderloin. Starting at the end closest to you, tightly roll the tenderloin like a jam roll. Tie the rolled tenderloin tightly with kitchen twine. 4. Place the meat in the air fryer basket and air fry for 5 minutes. Flip the meat over and cook for another 5

minutes, or until the internal temperature reaches 57°C for medium-rare. 5. To serve, smear a line of yellow mustard on a platter, then place the meat next to it and add halved cherry tomatoes on the side, if desired. Drizzle with olive oil and garnish with rosemary sprigs and lavender flowers, if desired. 6. Best served fresh. Store leftovers in an airtight container in the fridge for 3 days. Reheat in a preheated 180°C air fryer for 4 minutes, or until heated through.

Meat and Rice Stuffed Peppers

Prep time: 20 minutes | Cook time: 18 minutes | Serves 4

- ◆ 340 g lean beef mince
- ◆ 110 g lean pork mince
- ◆ 60 g onion, minced
- ◆ 1 (425 g) tin finely-chopped tomatoes
- ◆ 1 teaspoon Worcestershire sauce
- ◆ 1 teaspoon barbecue seasoning
- ◆ 1 teaspoon honey
- ◆ ½ teaspoon dried basil
- ◆ 120 g cooked brown rice
- ◆ ½ teaspoon garlic powder
- ◆ ½ teaspoon oregano
- ◆ ½ teaspoon salt
- ◆ 2 small peppers, cut in half, stems removed, deseeded
- ◆ Cooking spray

1. Preheat the air fryer to 180°C and spritz a baking tray with cooking spray. 2. Arrange the beef, pork, and onion in the baking tray and bake in the preheated air fryer for 8 minutes. Break the minced meat into chunks halfway through the cooking. 3. Meanwhile, combine the tomatoes, Worcestershire sauce, barbecue seasoning, honey, and basil in a saucepan. Stir to mix well. 4. Transfer the cooked meat mixture to a large bowl and add the cooked rice, garlic powder, oregano, salt, and 60 ml of the tomato mixture. Stir to mix well. 5. Stuff the pepper halves with the mixture, then arrange the pepper halves in the air fryer and air fry for 10 minutes or until the peppers are lightly charred. 6. Serve the stuffed peppers with the remaining tomato sauce on top.

Almond and Caraway Crust Steak

Prep time: 16 minutes | Cook time: 10 minutes | Serves 4

- ◆ 40 g almond flour
- ◆ 2 eggs
- ◆ 2 teaspoons caraway seeds
- ◆ 4 beef steaks
- ◆ 2 teaspoons garlic powder
- ◆ 1 tablespoon melted butter
- ◆ Fine sea salt and cayenne pepper, to taste

1. Generously coat steaks with garlic powder, caraway seeds, salt, and cayenne pepper. 2. In a mixing dish, thoroughly combine melted butter with seasoned crumbs. In another bowl, beat the eggs until they're well whisked. 3. First, coat steaks with the beaten egg; then, coat beef steaks with the buttered crumb mixture. Place the steaks in the air fryer basket; cook for 10 minutes at 180°C. Bon appétit!

Garlic Balsamic London Broil

Prep time: 30 minutes | Cook time: 8 to 10 minutes | Serves 8

- ◆ 900 g bavette or skirt steak
- ◆ 3 large garlic cloves, minced
- ◆ 3 tablespoons balsamic vinegar
- ◆ 3 tablespoons wholegrain mustard
- ◆ 2 tablespoons olive oil
- ◆ Sea salt and ground black pepper, to taste
- ◆ ½ teaspoon dried hot red pepper flakes

1. Score both sides of the cleaned steak. 2. Thoroughly combine the remaining ingredients; massage this mixture into the meat to coat it on all sides. Let it marinate for at least 3 hours. 3. Set the air fryer to 200°C; Then cook the steak for 15 minutes. Flip it over and cook another 10 to 12 minutes. Bon appétit!

Garlic-Marinated Bavette Steak

Prep time: 30 minutes | Cook time: 8 to 10 minutes | Serves 6

- ◆ 120 ml avocado oil
- ◆ 60 ml soy sauce or tamari
- ◆ 1 shallot, minced
- ◆ 1 tablespoon minced garlic
- ◆ 2 tablespoons chopped fresh oregano, or 2 teaspoons dried
- ◆ 1½ teaspoons sea salt
- ◆ 1 teaspoon freshly ground black pepper
- ◆ ¼ teaspoon red pepper flakes
- ◆ 900 g bavette or skirt steak

1. In a blender, combine the avocado oil, soy sauce, shallot, garlic, oregano, salt, black pepper, and red pepper flakes. Process until smooth. 2. Place the steak in a zip-top plastic bag or shallow dish with the marinade. Seal the bag or cover the dish and marinate in the refrigerator for at least 2 hours or overnight. 3. Remove the steak from the bag and discard the marinade. 4. Set the air fryer to 200°C. Place the steak in the air fryer basket (if needed, cut into sections and work in batches). Air fry for 4 to 6 minutes, flip the steak, and cook for another 4 minutes or until the internal temperature reaches 49°C in the thickest part for medium-rare (or as desired).

Smoky Pork Tenderloin

Prep time: 5 minutes | Cook time: 19 to 22 minutes | Serves 6

- ◆ 680 g pork tenderloin
- ◆ 1 tablespoon avocado oil
- ◆ 1 teaspoon chilli powder
- ◆ 1 teaspoon smoked paprika
- ◆ 1 teaspoon garlic powder
- ◆ 1 teaspoon sea salt
- ◆ 1 teaspoon freshly ground black pepper

1. Pierce the tenderloin all over with a fork and rub the oil all over the meat. 2. In a small dish, stir together the chilli powder, smoked paprika, garlic powder, salt, and pepper. 3. Rub the spice mixture all over the tenderloin. 4. Set the air fryer to 200°C. Place the pork in the air fryer basket and air fry for 10 minutes. Flip the tenderloin and cook for 9 to 12 minutes more, until an instant-read thermometer reads at least 64°C. 5. Allow the tenderloin to rest for 5 minutes, then slice and serve.

Garlic Butter Steak Bites

Prep time: 5 minutes | Cook time: 16 minutes | Serves 3

- ◆ Oil, for spraying
- ◆ 450 g boneless steak, cut into 1-inch pieces
- ◆ 2 tablespoons olive oil
- ◆ 1 teaspoon Worcestershire sauce
- ◆ ½ teaspoon granulated garlic
- ◆ ½ teaspoon salt
- ◆ ¼ teaspoon freshly ground black pepper

1. Preheat the air fryer to 200°C. Line the air fryer basket with parchment and spray lightly with oil. 2. In a medium bowl, combine the steak, olive oil, Worcestershire sauce, garlic, salt,

and black pepper and toss until evenly coated. 3. Place the steak in a single layer in the prepared basket. You may have to work in batches, depending on the size of your air fryer. 4. Cook for 10 to 16 minutes, flipping every 3 to 4 minutes. The total cooking time will depend on the thickness of the meat and your preferred doneness. If you want it well done, it may take up to 5 additional minutes.

Greek Lamb Rack

Prep time: 5 minutes | Cook time: 10 minutes | Serves 4

- ◆ 60 g freshly squeezed lemon juice
- ◆ 1 teaspoon oregano
- ◆ 2 teaspoons minced fresh rosemary
- ◆ 1 teaspoon minced fresh thyme
- ◆ 2 tablespoons minced garlic
- ◆ Salt and freshly ground black pepper, to taste
- ◆ 2 to 4 tablespoons olive oil
- ◆ 1 lamb rib rack (7 to 8 ribs)

1. Preheat the air fryer to 180°C. 2. In a small mixing bowl, combine the lemon juice, oregano, rosemary, thyme, garlic, salt, pepper, and olive oil and mix well. 3. Rub the mixture over the lamb, covering all the meat. Put the rack of lamb in the air fryer. Roast for 10 minutes. Flip the rack halfway through. 4. After 10 minutes, measure the internal temperature of the rack of lamb reaches at least 64°C. 5. Serve immediately.

Bacon-Wrapped Pork Tenderloin

Prep time: 30 minutes | Cook time: 22 to 25 minutes | Serves 6

- ◆ 120 g minced onion
- ◆ 120 ml apple cider, or apple juice
- ◆ 60 ml honey
- ◆ 1 tablespoon minced garlic
- ◆ ¼ teaspoon salt
- ◆ ¼ teaspoon freshly ground black pepper
- ◆ 900 g pork tenderloin
- ◆ 1 to 2 tablespoons oil
- ◆ 8 uncooked bacon slices

1. In a medium bowl, stir together the onion, cider, honey, garlic, salt, and pepper. Transfer to a large resealable bag or airtight container and add the pork. Seal the bag. Refrigerate to marinate for at least 2 hours. 2. Preheat the air fryer to 200°C. Line the air fryer basket with parchment paper. 3. Remove the

pork from the marinade and place it on the parchment. Spritz with oil. 4. Cook for 15 minutes. 5. Wrap the bacon slices around the pork and secure them with toothpicks. Turn the pork roast and spritz with oil. Cook for 7 to 10 minutes more until the internal temperature reaches 64ºC, depending on how well-done you like pork loin. It will continue cooking after it's removed from the fryer, so let it sit for 5 minutes before serving.

Spicy Rump Steak

Prep time: 25 minutes | Cook time: 12 to 18 minutes | Serves 4

◆ 2 tablespoons salsa

◆ 1 tablespoon minced chipotle pepper or chipotle paste

◆ 1 tablespoon apple cider vinegar

◆ 1 teaspoon ground cumin

◆ ⅛ teaspoon freshly ground black pepper

◆ ⅛ teaspoon red pepper flakes

◆ 340 g rump steak, cut into 4 pieces and gently pounded to about ⅓ inch thick

◆ Cooking oil spray

1. In a small bowl, thoroughly mix the salsa, chipotle pepper, vinegar, cumin, black pepper, and red pepper flakes. Rub this mixture into both sides of each steak piece. Let stand for 15 minutes at room temperature. 2. Insert the crisper plate into the basket and place the basket into the unit. Preheat the unit by selecting AIR FRY, setting the temperature to 200ºC, and setting the time to 3 minutes. Select START/STOP to begin. 3. Once the unit is preheated, spray the crisper plate with cooking oil. Working in batches, place 2 steaks into the basket. 4. Select AIR FRY, set the temperature to 200ºC, and set the time to 9 minutes. Select START/STOP to begin. 5. After about 6 minutes, check the steaks. If a food thermometer inserted into the meat registers at least 64ºC, they are done. If not, resume cooking. 6. When the cooking is done, transfer the steaks to a clean plate and cover with aluminium foil to keep warm. Repeat steps 3, 4, and 5 with the remaining steaks. 7. Thinly slice the steaks against the grain and serve.

Herb-Roasted Beef Tips with Onions

Prep time: 5 minutes | Cook time: 10 minutes | Serves 4

◆ 450 g rib eye steak, cubed

◆ 2 garlic cloves, minced

◆ 2 tablespoons olive oil

◆ 1 tablespoon fresh oregano

◆ 1 teaspoon salt

◆ ½ teaspoon black pepper

◆ 1 brown onion, thinly sliced

1. Preheat the air fryer to 190ºC. 2. In a medium bowl, combine the steak, garlic, olive oil, oregano, salt, pepper, and onion. Mix until all of the beef and onion are well coated. 3. Put the seasoned steak mixture into the air fryer basket. Roast for 5 minutes. Stir and roast for 5 minutes more. 4. Let rest for 5 minutes before serving with some favourite sides.

Buttery Pork Chops

Prep time: 5 minutes | Cook time: 12 minutes | Serves 4

◆ 4 (110 g) boneless pork chops

◆ ½ teaspoon salt

◆ ¼ teaspoon ground black pepper

◆ 2 tablespoons salted butter, softened

1. Sprinkle pork chops on all sides with salt and pepper. Place chops into ungreased air fryer basket in a single layer. Adjust the temperature to 200ºC and air fry for 12 minutes. Pork chops will be golden and have an internal temperature of at least 64ºC when done. 2. Use tongs to remove cooked pork chops from air fryer and place onto a large plate. Top each chop with ½ tablespoon butter and let sit 2 minutes to melt. Serve warm.

Pigs in a Blanket

Prep time: 10 minutes | Cook time: 7 minutes | Serves 2

◆ 120 g shredded Mozzarella cheese

◆ 2 tablespoons blanched finely ground almond flour

◆ 30 g full-fat cream cheese

◆ 2 (110 g) beef smoked banger, cut in two

◆ ½ teaspoon sesame seeds

1. Place Mozzarella, almond flour, and cream cheese in a large microwave-safe bowl. Microwave for 45 seconds and stir until smooth. Roll dough into a ball and cut in half. 2. Press each half out into a 4 × 5-inch rectangle. Roll one banger up in each dough half and press seams closed. Sprinkle the top with sesame seeds. 3. Place each wrapped banger into the air fryer

basket. 4. Adjust the temperature to 200°C and air fry for 7 minutes. 5. The outside will be golden when completely cooked. Serve immediately.

Spice-Coated Steaks with Cucumber and Snap Pea Salad

Prep time: 15 minutes | Cook time: 15 to 20 minutes | Serves 4

◆ 1 (680 g) boneless rump steak, trimmed and halved crosswise

◆ 1½ teaspoons chilli powder

◆ 1½ teaspoons ground cumin

◆ ¾ teaspoon ground coriander

◆ ⅛ teaspoon cayenne pepper

◆ ⅛ teaspoon ground cinnamon

◆ 1¼ teaspoons plus ⅛ teaspoon salt, divided

◆ ½ teaspoon plus ⅛ teaspoon ground black pepper, divided

◆ 1 teaspoon plus 1½ tablespoons extra-virgin olive oil, divided

◆ 3 tablespoons mayonnaise

◆ 1½ tablespoons white wine vinegar

◆ 1 tablespoon minced fresh dill

◆ 1 small garlic clove, minced

◆ 230 g sugar snap peas, strings removed and cut in half on bias

◆ ½ cucumber, halved lengthwise and sliced thin

◆ 2 radishes, trimmed, halved and sliced thin

◆ 475 g baby rocket

1. Preheat the air fryer to 200°C. 2. In a bowl, mix chilli powder, cumin, coriander, cayenne pepper, cinnamon, 1¼ teaspoons salt and ½ teaspoon pepper until well combined. 3. Add the steaks to another bowl and pat dry with paper towels. Brush with 1 teaspoon oil and transfer to the bowl of spice mixture. Roll over to coat thoroughly. 4. Arrange the coated steaks in the air fryer basket, spaced evenly apart. Air fry for 15 to 20 minutes, or until an instant-read thermometer inserted in the thickest part of the meat registers at least 64°C. Flip halfway through to ensure even cooking. 5. Transfer the steaks to a clean work surface and wrap with aluminium foil. Let stand while preparing salad. 6. Make the salad: In a large bowl, stir together 1½ tablespoons olive oil, mayonnaise, vinegar, dill, garlic, ⅛ teaspoon salt, and ⅛ teaspoon pepper. Add snap peas, cucumber, radishes and rocket. Toss to blend well. 7. Slice the steaks and serve with the salad.

CHAPTER 6 Poultry and Meat

Chicken Chimichangas

Prep time: 20 minutes | Cook time: 8 to 10 minutes |

Serves 4

- 280 g cooked chicken, shredded
- 2 tablespoons chopped green chilies
- ½ teaspoon oregano
- ½ teaspoon cumin
- ½ teaspoon onion powder
- ¼ teaspoon garlic powder
- Salt and pepper, to taste
- 8 flour tortillas (6- or 7-inch diameter)
- Oil for misting or cooking spray
- Chimichanga Sauce:
- 2 tablespoons butter
- 2 tablespoons flour
- 235 ml chicken broth
- 60 g light sour cream
- ¼ teaspoon salt
- 60 g Pepper Jack or Monterey Jack cheese, shredded

1. Make the sauce by melting butter in a saucepan over medium-low heat. Stir in flour until smooth and slightly bubbly. Gradually add broth, stirring constantly until smooth. Cook and stir 1 minute, until the mixture slightly thickens. Remove from heat and stir in sour cream and salt. Set aside. 2. In a medium bowl, mix together the chicken, chilies, oregano, cumin, onion powder, garlic, salt, and pepper. Stir in 3 to 4 tablespoons of the sauce, using just enough to make the filling moist but not soupy. 3. Divide filling among the 8 corn wraps. Place filling down the centre of maize wrap, stopping about 1 inch from edges. Fold one side of maize wrap over filling, fold the two sides in, and then roll up. Mist all sides with oil or cooking spray. 4. Place chimichangas in air fryer basket seam side down. To fit more into the basket, you tin stand them on their sides with the seams against the sides of the basket. 5. Air fry at 180°C for 8 to 10 minutes or until heated through and crispy brown outside. 6. Add the shredded cheese to the remaining sauce. Stir over low heat, warming just until the cheese melts. Don't boil or sour cream may curdle. 7. Drizzle the sauce over the chimichangas.

Chicken Croquettes with Creole Sauce

Prep time: 30 minutes | Cook time: 10 minutes |

Serves 4

- 280 g shredded cooked chicken
- 120 g shredded Cheddar cheese
- 2 eggs
- 15 g finely chopped onion
- 15 g ground almonds
- 1 tablespoon poultry seasoning
- Olive oil
- Creole Sauce:
- 60 g mayonnaise
- 60 g sour cream
- 1½ teaspoons Dijon mustard
- 1½ teaspoons fresh lemon juice
- ½ teaspoon garlic powder
- ½ teaspoon Creole seasoning

1. In a large bowl, combine the chicken, Cheddar, eggs, onion, ground almonds, and poultry seasoning. Stir gently until thoroughly combined. Cover and refrigerate for 30 minutes. 2. Meanwhile, to make the Creole sauce: In a small bowl, whisk together the mayonnaise, sour cream, Dijon mustard, lemon juice, garlic powder, and Creole seasoning until thoroughly combined. Cover and refrigerate until ready to serve. 3. Preheat the air fryer to 200°C. Divide the chicken mixture into 8 portions and shape into patties. 4. Working in batches if necessary, arrange the patties in a single layer in the air fryer basket and coat both sides lightly with olive oil. Pausing halfway through the cooking time to flip the patties, air fry for 10 minutes, or until lightly browned and the cheese is melted. Serve with the Creole sauce.

Israeli Chicken Schnitzel

Prep time: 5 minutes | Cook time: 10 minutes | Serves 4

- 2 large boneless, skinless chicken breasts, each weighing about 450 g
- 65 g plain flour

- ◆ 2 teaspoons garlic powder
- ◆ 2 teaspoons kosher salt
- ◆ 1 teaspoon black pepper
- ◆ 1 teaspoon paprika
- ◆ 2 eggs beaten with 2 tablespoons water
- ◆ 125 g panko bread crumbs
- ◆ Vegetable oil spray
- ◆ Lemon juice, for serving

1. Preheat the air fryer to 190°C. 2. Place 1 chicken breast between 2 pieces of cling film. Use a mallet or a rolling pin to pound the chicken until it is ¼ inch thick. Set aside. Repeat with the second breast. Whisk together the flour, garlic powder, salt, pepper, and paprika on a large plate. Place the panko in a separate shallow bowl or pie plate. 3. Dredge 1 chicken breast in the flour, shaking off any excess, then dip it in the egg mixture. Dredge the chicken breast in the panko, making sure to coat it completely. Shake off any excess panko. Place the battered chicken breast on a plate. Repeat with the second chicken breast. 4. Spray the air fryer basket with oil spray. Place 1 of the battered chicken breasts in the basket and spray the top with oil spray. Air fry until the top is browned, about 5 minutes. Flip the chicken and spray the second side with oil spray. Air fry until the second side is browned and crispy and the internal temperature reaches 76°C. Remove the first chicken breast from the air fryer and repeat with the second chicken breast. 5. Serve hot with lemon juice.

Golden Chicken Cutlets

Prep time: 15 minutes | Cook time: 15 minutes | Serves 4

- ◆ 2 tablespoons panko breadcrumbs
- ◆ 20 g grated Parmesan cheese
- ◆ ⅛ tablespoon paprika
- ◆ ½ tablespoon garlic powder
- ◆ 2 large eggs
- ◆ 4 chicken cutlets
- ◆ 1 tablespoon parsley
- ◆ Salt and ground black pepper, to taste
- ◆ Cooking spray

1. Preheat air fryer to 200°C. Spritz the air fryer basket with cooking spray. 2. Combine the breadcrumbs, Parmesan, paprika, garlic powder, salt, and ground black pepper in a large bowl. Stir to mix well. Beat the eggs in a separate bowl. 3. Dredge the chicken cutlets in the beaten eggs, then roll over the breadcrumbs mixture to coat well. Shake the excess off. 4. Transfer the chicken cutlets in the preheated air fryer and spritz with cooking spray. 5. Air fry for 15 minutes or until crispy and golden brown. Flip the cutlets halfway through. 6. Serve with parsley on top.

Butter and Bacon Chicken

Prep time: 10 minutes | Cook time: 65 minutes | Serves 6

1 (1.8 kg) whole chicken

- ◆ 2 tablespoons salted butter, softened
- ◆ 1 teaspoon dried thyme
- ◆ ½ teaspoon garlic powder
- ◆ 1 teaspoon salt
- ◆ ½ teaspoon ground black pepper
- ◆ 6 slices sugar-free bacon

1. Pat chicken dry with a paper towel, then rub with butter on all sides. Sprinkle thyme, garlic powder, salt, and pepper over chicken. 2. Place chicken into ungreased air fryer basket, breast side up. Lay strips of bacon over chicken and secure with toothpicks. 3. Adjust the temperature to 180°C and air fry for 65 minutes. Halfway through cooking, remove and set aside bacon and flip chicken over. Chicken will be done when the skin is golden and crispy and the internal temperature is at least 76°C. Serve warm with bacon.

Chicken Parmesan

Prep time: 15 minutes | Cook time: 10 minutes | Serves 4

- ◆ Oil, for spraying
- ◆ 2 (230 g) boneless, skinless chicken breasts
- ◆ 60 g Italian-style bread crumbs
- ◆ 20 g grated Parmesan cheese, plus 45 g shredded
- ◆ 4 tablespoons unsalted butter, melted
- ◆ 115 g marinara sauce

1. Preheat the air fryer to 180°C. Line the air fryer basket with parchment and spray lightly with oil. 2. Cut each chicken breast in half through its thickness to make 4 thin cutlets. Using a meat tenderizer, pound each cutlet until it is about ¾ inch thick. 3. On a plate, mix together the bread crumbs and grated Parmesan cheese. 4. Lightly brush the chicken with the melted butter, then dip into the bread crumb mixture. 5. Place the chicken in the prepared basket and spray lightly with oil. You may need to work in batches, depending on the size of your air

fryer. 6. Cook for 6 minutes. Top the chicken with the marinara and shredded Parmesan cheese, dividing evenly. Cook for another 3 to 4 minutes, or until golden brown, crispy, and the internal temperature reaches 76ºC.

Peachy Chicken Chunks with Cherries

Prep time: 8 minutes | Cook time: 14 to 16 minutes | Serves 4

◆ 100 g peach preserves

◆ 1 teaspoon ground rosemary

◆ ½ teaspoon black pepper

◆ ½ teaspoon salt

◆ ½ teaspoon marjoram

◆ 1 teaspoon light olive oil

◆ 450 g boneless chicken breasts, cut in 1½-inch chunks

◆ Oil for misting or cooking spray

◆ 1 (280 g) package frozen unsweetened dark cherries, thawed and drained

1. In a medium bowl, mix together peach preserves, rosemary, pepper, salt, marjoram, and olive oil. 2. Stir in chicken chunks and toss to coat well with the preserve mixture. 3. Spray the air fryer basket with oil or cooking spray and lay chicken chunks in basket. 4. Air fry at 200ºC for 7 minutes. Stir. Cook for 6 to 8 more minutes or until chicken juices run clear. 5. When chicken has cooked through, scatter the cherries over and cook for additional minute to heat cherries.

Simply Terrific Turkey Meatballs

Prep time: 10 minutes | Cook time: 7 to 10 minutes | Serves 4

◆ 1 red pepper, seeded and coarsely chopped

◆ 2 cloves garlic, coarsely chopped

◆ 15 g chopped fresh parsley

◆ 680 g 85% lean turkey mince

◆ 1 egg, lightly beaten

◆ 45 g grated Parmesan cheese

◆ 1 teaspoon salt

◆ ½ teaspoon freshly ground black pepper

1. Preheat the air fryer to 200ºC. 2. In a food processor fitted with a metal blade, combine the pepper, garlic, and parsley. Pulse until finely chopped. Transfer the vegetables to a large mixing bowl. 3. Add the turkey, egg, Parmesan, salt, and black

pepper. Mix gently until thoroughly combined. Shape the mixture into 1¼-inch meatballs. 4. Working in batches if necessary, arrange the meatballs in a single layer in the air fryer basket; coat lightly with olive oil spray. Pausing halfway through the cooking time to shake the basket, air fry for 7 to 10 minutes, until lightly browned and a thermometer inserted into the centre of a meatball registers 76ºC.

African Merguez Meatballs

Prep time: 30 minutes | Cook time: 10 minutes | Serves 4

◆ 450 g chicken mince

◆ 2 garlic cloves, finely minced

◆ 1 tablespoon sweet Hungarian paprika

◆ 1 teaspoon kosher salt

◆ 1 teaspoon sugar

◆ 1 teaspoon ground cumin

◆ ½ teaspoon black pepper

◆ ½ teaspoon ground fennel

◆ ½ teaspoon ground coriander

◆ ½ teaspoon cayenne pepper

◆ ¼ teaspoon ground allspice

1. In a large bowl, gently mix the chicken, garlic, paprika, salt, sugar, cumin, black pepper, fennel, coriander, cayenne, and allspice until all the ingredients are incorporated. Let stand for 30 minutes at room temperature, or cover and refrigerate for up to 24 hours. 2. Form the mixture into 16 meatballs. Arrange them in a single layer in the air fryer basket. Set the air fryer to 200ºC for 10 minutes, turning the meatballs halfway through the cooking time. Use a meat thermometer to ensure the meatballs have reached an internal temperature of 76ºC.

Apricot-Glazed Chicken Drumsticks

Prep time: 15 minutes | Cook time: 30 minutes | Makes 6 drumsticks

◆ For the Glaze:

◆ 160 g apricot preserves

◆ ½ teaspoon tamari

◆ ¼ teaspoon chilli powder

◆ 2 teaspoons Dijon mustard

◆ For the Chicken:

◆ 6 chicken drumsticks

◆ ½ teaspoon seasoning salt

- 1 teaspoon salt
- ½ teaspoon ground black pepper
- Cooking spray

Make the glaze: 1. Combine the ingredients for the glaze in a saucepan, then heat over low heat for 10 minutes or until thickened. 2. Turn off the heat and sit until ready to use. Make the Chicken: 1. Preheat the air fryer to 190ºC. Spritz the air fryer basket with cooking spray. 2. Combine the seasoning salt, salt, and pepper in a small bowl. Stir to mix well. 3. Place the chicken drumsticks in the preheated air fryer. Spritz with cooking spray and sprinkle with the salt mixture on both sides. 4. Air fry for 20 minutes or until well browned. Flip the chicken halfway through. 5. Baste the chicken with the glaze and air fryer for 2 more minutes or until the chicken tenderloin is glossy. 6. Serve immediately.

Thai Curry Meatballs

Prep time: 10 minutes | Cook time: 10 minutes | Serves 4

- 450 g chicken mince
- 15 g chopped fresh coriander
- 1 teaspoon chopped fresh mint
- 1 tablespoon fresh lime juice
- 1 tablespoon Thai red, green, or yellow curry paste
- 1 tablespoon fish sauce
- 2 garlic cloves, minced
- 2 teaspoons minced fresh ginger
- ½ teaspoon kosher salt
- ½ teaspoon black pepper
- ¼ teaspoon red pepper flakes

1. Preheat the air fryer to 200ºC. 2. In a large bowl, gently mix the chicken mince, coriander, mint, lime juice, curry paste, fish sauce, garlic, ginger, salt, black pepper, and red pepper flakes until thoroughly combined. 3. Form the mixture into 16 meatballs. Place the meatballs in a single layer in the air fryer basket. Air fry for 10 minutes, turning the meatballs halfway through the cooking time. Use a meat thermometer to ensure the meatballs have reached an internal temperature of 76ºC. Serve immediately.

Fried Chicken Breasts

Prep time: 30 minutes | Cook time: 12 to 14 minutes | Serves 4

- 450 g boneless, skinless chicken breasts

- 180 ml dill gherkin juice
- 35 g finely ground blanched almond flour
- 70 g finely grated Parmesan cheese
- ½ teaspoon sea salt
- ½ teaspoon freshly ground black pepper
- 2 large eggs
- Avocado oil spray

1. Place the chicken breasts in a zip-top bag or between two pieces of cling film. Using a meat mallet or heavy frying pan, pound the chicken to a uniform ½-inch thickness. 2. Place the chicken in a large bowl with the gherkin juice. Cover and allow to brine in the refrigerator for up to 2 hours. 3. In a shallow dish, combine the almond flour, Parmesan cheese, salt, and pepper. In a separate, shallow bowl, beat the eggs. 4. Drain the chicken and pat it dry with paper towels. Dip in the eggs and then in the flour mixture, making sure to press the coating into the chicken. Spray both sides of the coated breasts with oil. 5. Spray the air fryer basket with oil and put the chicken inside. Set the temperature to 200ºC and air fry for 6 to 7 minutes. 6. Carefully flip the breasts with a spatula. Spray the breasts again with oil and continue cooking for 6 to 7 minutes more, until golden and crispy.

Cajun-Breaded Chicken Bites

Prep time: 10 minutes | Cook time: 12 minutes | Serves 4

- 450 g boneless, skinless chicken breasts, cut into 1-inch cubes
- 120 g heavy whipping cream
- ½ teaspoon salt
- ¼ teaspoon ground black pepper
- 30 g plain pork rinds, finely crushed
- 40 g unflavoured whey protein powder
- ½ teaspoon Cajun seasoning

1. Place chicken in a medium bowl and pour in cream. Stir to coat. Sprinkle with salt and pepper. 2. In a separate large bowl, combine pork rinds, protein powder, and Cajun seasoning. Remove chicken from cream, shaking off any excess, and toss in dry mix until fully coated. 3. Place bites into ungreased air fryer basket. Adjust the temperature to 200ºC and air fry for 12 minutes, shaking the basket twice during cooking. Bites will be done when golden brown and have an internal temperature of at least 76ºC. Serve warm.

Turkish Chicken Kebabs

Prep time: 30 minutes | Cook time: 15 minutes | Serves 4

- 70 g plain Greek yoghurt
- 1 tablespoon minced garlic
- 1 tablespoon tomato paste
- 1 tablespoon fresh lemon juice
- 1 tablespoon vegetable oil
- 1 teaspoon kosher salt
- 1 teaspoon ground cumin
- 1 teaspoon sweet Hungarian paprika
- ½ teaspoon ground cinnamon
- ½ teaspoon black pepper
- ½ teaspoon cayenne pepper
- 450 g boneless, skinless chicken thighs, quartered crosswise

1. In a large bowl, combine the yoghurt, garlic, tomato paste, lemon juice, vegetable oil, salt, cumin, paprika, cinnamon, black pepper, and cayenne. Stir until the spices are blended into the yoghurt. 2. Add the chicken to the bowl and toss until well coated. Marinate at room temperature for 30 minutes, or cover and refrigerate for up to 24 hours. 3. Arrange the chicken in a single layer in the air fryer basket. Set the air fryer to (190°C for 10 minutes. Turn the chicken and cook for 5 minutes more. Use a meat thermometer to ensure the chicken has reached an internal temperature of 76°C.

Chicken Wings with Piri Piri Sauce

Prep time: 30 minutes | Cook time: 30 minutes | Serves 6

- 12 chicken wings
- 45 g butter, melted
- 1 teaspoon onion powder
- ½ teaspoon cumin powder
- 1 teaspoon garlic paste
- Sauce:
- 60 g piri piri peppers, stemmed and chopped
- 1 tablespoon pimiento, seeded and minced
- 1 garlic clove, chopped
- 2 tablespoons fresh lemon juice
- ⅓ teaspoon sea salt
- ½ teaspoon tarragon

1. Steam the chicken wings using a steamer basket that is placed over a saucepan with boiling water; reduce the heat. 2. Now, steam the wings for 10 minutes over a moderate heat. Toss the wings with butter, onion powder, cumin powder, and garlic paste. 3. Let the chicken wings cool to room temperature. Then, refrigerate them for 45 to 50 minutes. 4. Roast in the preheated air fryer at 170°C for 25 to 30 minutes; make sure to flip them halfway through. 5. While the chicken wings are cooking, prepare the sauce by mixing all of the sauce ingredients in a food processor. Toss the wings with prepared Piri Piri Sauce and serve.

Potato-Crusted Chicken

Prep time: 15 minutes | Cook time: 22 to 25 minutes | Serves 4

- 60 g buttermilk
- 1 large egg, beaten
- 180 g instant potato flakes
- 20 g grated Parmesan cheese
- 1 teaspoon salt
- ½ teaspoon freshly ground black pepper
- 2 whole boneless, skinless chicken breasts (about 450 g each), halved
- 1 to 2 tablespoons oil

1. In a shallow bowl, whisk the buttermilk and egg until blended. In another shallow bowl, stir together the potato flakes, cheese, salt, and pepper. 2. One at a time, dip the chicken pieces in the buttermilk mixture and the potato flake mixture, coating thoroughly. 3. Preheat the air fryer to 200°C. Line the air fryer basket with parchment paper. 4. Place the coated chicken on the parchment and spritz with oil. 5. Cook for 15 minutes. Flip the chicken, spritz it with oil, and cook for 7 to 10 minutes more until the outside is crispy and the inside is no longer pink.

Chicken Breasts with Asparagus, Beans, and Rocket

Prep time: 20 minutes | Cook time: 25 minutes | Serves 2

- 160 g canned cannellini beans, rinsed
- 1½ tablespoons red wine vinegar
- 1 garlic clove, minced
- 2 tablespoons extra-virgin olive oil, divided
- Salt and ground black pepper, to taste
- ½ red onion, sliced thinly

- 230 g asparagus, trimmed and cut into 1-inch lengths
- 2 (230 g) boneless, skinless chicken breasts, trimmed
- ¼ teaspoon paprika
- ½ teaspoon ground coriander
- 60 g baby rocket, rinsed and drained

1. Preheat the air fryer to 200°C. 2. Warm the beans in microwave for 1 minutes and combine with red wine vinegar, garlic, 1 tablespoon of olive oil, ¼ teaspoon of salt, and ¼ teaspoon of ground black pepper in a bowl. Stir to mix well. 3. Combine the onion with ⅛ teaspoon of salt, ⅛ teaspoon of ground black pepper, and 2 teaspoons of olive oil in a separate bowl. Toss to coat well. 4. Place the onion in the air fryer and air fry for 2 minutes, then add the asparagus and air fry for 8 more minutes or until the asparagus is tender. Shake the basket halfway through. Transfer the onion and asparagus to the bowl with beans. Set aside. 5. Toss the chicken breasts with remaining ingredients, except for the baby rocket, in a large bowl. 6. Put the chicken breasts in the air fryer and air fry for 14 minutes or until the internal temperature of the chicken reaches at least 76°C. Flip the breasts halfway through. 7. Remove the chicken from the air fryer and serve on an aluminium foil with asparagus, beans, onion, and rocket. Sprinkle with salt and ground black pepper. Toss to serve.

Chicken Rochambeau

Prep time: 15 minutes | Cook time: 20 minutes | Serves 4

- 1 tablespoon butter
- 4 chicken tenders, cut in half crosswise
- Salt and pepper, to taste
- 15 g flour
- Oil for misting
- 4 slices gammon, ¼- to ⅜-inches thick and large enough to cover an English muffin
- 2 English muffins, split
- Sauce:
- 2 tablespoons butter
- 25 g chopped spring onions
- 50 g chopped mushrooms
- 2 tablespoons flour
- 240 ml chicken broth
- ¼ teaspoon garlic powder

- 1½ teaspoons Worcestershire sauce

1. Place 1 tablespoon of butter in a baking pan and air fry at 200°C for 2 minutes to melt. 2. Sprinkle chicken tenders with salt and pepper to taste, then roll in the flour. 3. Place chicken in baking pan, turning pieces to coat with melted butter. 4. Air fry at 200°C for 5 minutes. Turn chicken pieces over, and spray tops lightly with olive oil. Cook 5 minutes longer or until juices run clear. The chicken will not brown. 5. While chicken is cooking, make the sauce: In a medium saucepan, melt the 2 tablespoons of butter. 6. Add onions and mushrooms and sauté until tender, about 3 minutes. 7. Stir in the flour. Gradually add broth, stirring constantly until you have a smooth gravy. 8. Add garlic powder and Worcestershire sauce and simmer on low heat until sauce thickens, about 5 minutes. 9. When chicken is cooked, remove baking pan from air fryer and set aside. 10. Place gammon slices directly into air fryer basket and air fry at 200°C for 5 minutes or until hot and beginning to sizzle a little. Remove and set aside on top of the chicken for now. 11. Place the English muffin halves in air fryer basket and air fry at 200°C for 1 minute. 12. Open air fryer and place a gammon slice on top of each English muffin half. Stack 2 pieces of chicken on top of each gammon slice. Air fry for 1 to 2 minutes to heat through. 13. Place each English muffin stack on a serving plate and top with plenty of sauce.

Lemon Chicken with Garlic

Prep time: 5 minutes | Cook time: 20 to 25 minutes | Serves 4

- 8 bone-in chicken thighs, skin on
- 1 tablespoon olive oil
- 1½ teaspoons lemon-pepper seasoning
- ½ teaspoon paprika
- ½ teaspoon garlic powder
- ¼ teaspoon freshly ground black pepper
- Juice of ½ lemon

1. Preheat the air fryer to 180°C. 2. Place the chicken in a large bowl and drizzle with the olive oil. Top with the lemon-pepper seasoning, paprika, garlic powder, and freshly ground black pepper. Toss until thoroughly coated. 3. Working in batches if necessary, arrange the chicken in a single layer in the basket of the air fryer. Pausing halfway through the cooking time to turn the chicken, air fry for 20 to 25 minutes, until a thermometer inserted into the thickest piece registers 76°C. 4. Transfer the chicken to a serving platter and squeeze the lemon juice over

the top.

Jerk Chicken Thighs

Prep time: 30 minutes | Cook time: 15 to 20 minutes | Serves 6

- 2 teaspoons ground coriander
- 1 teaspoon ground allspice
- 1 teaspoon cayenne pepper
- 1 teaspoon ground ginger
- 1 teaspoon salt
- 1 teaspoon dried thyme
- ½ teaspoon ground cinnamon
- ½ teaspoon ground nutmeg
- 900 g boneless chicken thighs, skin on
- 2 tablespoons olive oil

1. In a small bowl, combine the coriander, allspice, cayenne, ginger, salt, thyme, cinnamon, and nutmeg. Stir until thoroughly combined. 2. Place the chicken in a baking dish and use paper towels to pat dry. Thoroughly coat both sides of the chicken with the spice mixture. Cover and refrigerate for at least 2 hours, preferably overnight. 3. Preheat the air fryer to 180ºC. 4. Working in batches if necessary, arrange the chicken in a single layer in the air fryer basket and lightly coat with the olive oil. Pausing halfway through the cooking time to flip the chicken, air fry for 15 to 20 minutes, until a thermometer inserted into the thickest part registers 76ºC.

Chicken Schnitzel

Prep time: 15 minutes | Cook time: 5 minutes | Serves 4

- 30 g plain flour
- 1 teaspoon marjoram
- ½ teaspoon thyme
- 1 teaspoon dried parsley flakes
- ½ teaspoon salt
- 1 egg
- 1 teaspoon lemon juice
- 1 teaspoon water
- 60 g breadcrumbs
- 4 chicken tenders, pounded thin, cut in half lengthwise
- Cooking spray

1. Preheat the air fryer to 200ºC and spritz with cooking spray. 2. Combine the flour, marjoram, thyme, parsley, and salt in a shallow dish. Stir to mix well. 3. Whisk the egg with lemon juice and water in a large bowl. Pour the breadcrumbs in a separate shallow dish. 4. Roll the chicken halves in the flour mixture first, then in the egg mixture, and then roll over the breadcrumbs to coat well. Shake the excess off. 5. Arrange the chicken halves in the preheated air fryer and spritz with cooking spray on both sides. 6. Air fry for 5 minutes or until the chicken halves are golden brown and crispy. Flip the halves halfway through. 7. Serve immediately.

Hawaiian Huli Huli Chicken

Prep time: 30 minutes | Cook time: 15 minutes | Serves 4

- 4 boneless, skinless chicken thighs (680 g)
- 1 (230 g) tin pineapple chunks in juice, drained, 60 ml juice reserved
- 60 ml soy sauce
- 25 g sugar
- 2 tablespoons ketchup
- 1 tablespoon minced fresh ginger
- 1 tablespoon minced garlic
- 25 g chopped spring onions

1. Use a fork to pierce the chicken all over to allow the marinade to penetrate better. Place the chicken in a large bowl or large resealable plastic bag. 2. Set the drained pineapple chunks aside. In a small microwave-safe bowl, combine the pineapple juice, soy sauce, sugar, ketchup, ginger, and garlic. Pour half the sauce over the chicken; toss to coat. Reserve the remaining sauce. Marinate the chicken at room temperature for 30 minutes, or cover and refrigerate for up to 24 hours. 3. Place the chicken in the air fryer basket. (Discard marinade.) Set the air fryer to 180ºC for 15 minutes, turning halfway through the cooking time. 4. Meanwhile, microwave the reserved sauce on high for 45 to 60 seconds, stirring every 15 seconds, until the sauce has the consistency of a thick glaze. 5. At the end of the cooking time, use a meat thermometer to ensure the chicken has reached an internal temperature of 76ºC. 6. Transfer the chicken to a serving platter. Pour the sauce over the chicken. Garnish with the pineapple chunks and spring onions.

Chicken Pesto Pizzas

Prep time: 10 minutes | Cook time: 12 minutes | Serves 4

- 450 g chicken mince thighs

- ¼ teaspoon salt
- ⅛ teaspoon ground black pepper
- 20 g basil pesto
- 225 g shredded Mozzarella cheese
- 4 grape tomatoes, sliced

1. Cut four squares of parchment paper to fit into your air fryer basket. 2. Place chicken mince in a large bowl and mix with salt and pepper. Divide mixture into four equal sections. 3. Wet your hands with water to prevent sticking, then press each section into a 6-inch circle onto a piece of ungreased parchment. Place each chicken crust into air fryer basket, working in batches if needed. 4. Adjust the temperature to 180°C and air fry for 10 minutes, turning crusts halfway through cooking. 5. Spread 1 tablespoon pesto across the top of each crust, then sprinkle with ¼ of the Mozzarella and top with 1 sliced tomato. Continue cooking at 180°C for 2 minutes. Cheese will be melted and brown when done. Serve warm.

Pork Rind Fried Chicken

Prep time: 30 minutes | Cook time: 20 minutes |
Serves 4

- 60 ml buffalo sauce
- 4 (115 g) boneless, skinless chicken breasts
- ½ teaspoon paprika
- ½ teaspoon garlic powder
- ¼ teaspoon ground black pepper
- 60 g g plain pork rinds, finely crushed

1. Pour buffalo sauce into a large sealable bowl or bag. Add chicken and toss to coat. Place sealed bowl or bag into refrigerator and let marinate at least 30 minutes up to overnight. 2. Remove chicken from marinade but do not shake excess sauce off chicken. Sprinkle both sides of thighs with paprika, garlic powder, and pepper. 3. Place pork rinds into a large bowl and press each chicken breast into pork rinds to coat evenly on both sides. 4. Place chicken into ungreased air fryer basket. Adjust the temperature to 200°C and roast for 20 minutes, turning chicken halfway through cooking. Chicken will be golden and have an internal temperature of at least 76°C when done. Serve warm.

Garlic Dill Wings

Prep time: 5 minutes | Cook time: 25 minutes | Serves 4

- 900 g bone-in chicken wings, separated at joints

- ½ teaspoon salt
- ½ teaspoon ground black pepper
- ½ teaspoon onion powder
- ½ teaspoon garlic powder
- 1 teaspoon dried dill

1. In a large bowl, toss wings with salt, pepper, onion powder, garlic powder, and dill until evenly coated. Place wings into ungreased air fryer basket in a single layer, working in batches if needed. 2. Adjust the temperature to 200°C and air fry for 25 minutes, shaking the basket every 7 minutes during cooking. Wings should have an internal temperature of at least 76°C and be golden brown when done. Serve warm.

Peanut Butter Chicken Satay

Prep time: 12 minutes | Cook time: 12 to 18 minutes |
Serves 4

- 120 g crunchy peanut butter
- 80 ml chicken broth
- 3 tablespoons low-sodium soy sauce
- 2 tablespoons freshly squeezed lemon juice
- 2 garlic cloves, minced
- 2 tablespoons extra-virgin olive oil
- 1 teaspoon curry powder
- 450 g chicken tenders
- Cooking oil spray

1. In a medium bowl, whisk the peanut butter, broth, soy sauce, lemon juice, garlic, olive oil, and curry powder until smooth. 2. Place 2 tablespoons of this mixture into a small bowl. Transfer the remaining sauce to a serving bowl and set aside. 3. Add the chicken tenders to the bowl with the 2 tablespoons of sauce and stir to coat. Let stand for a few minutes to marinate. 4. Insert the crisper plate into the basket and the basket into the unit. Preheat the unit by selecting AIR FRY, setting the temperature to 200°C, and setting the time to 3 minutes. Select START/STOP to begin. 5. Run a 6-inch bamboo skewer lengthwise through each chicken tender. 6. Once the unit is preheated, spray the crisper plate with cooking oil. Working in batches, place half the chicken skewers into the basket in a single layer without overlapping. 7. Select AIR FRY, set the temperature to 200°C, and set the time to 9 minutes. Select START/STOP to begin. 8. After 6 minutes, check the chicken. If a food thermometer inserted into the chicken registers 76°C, it is done. If not, resume cooking. 9. Repeat steps 6, 7, and 8 with the remaining chicken. 10. When the cooking is complete, serve

the chicken with the reserved sauce.

Garlic Parmesan Drumsticks

Prep time: 5 minutes | Cook time: 25 minutes | Serves 4

- ◆ 8 (115 g) chicken drumsticks
- ◆ ½ teaspoon salt
- ◆ ⅛ teaspoon ground black pepper
- ◆ ½ teaspoon garlic powder
- ◆ 2 tablespoons salted butter, melted
- ◆ 45 g grated Parmesan cheese
- ◆ 1 tablespoon dried parsley

1. Sprinkle drumsticks with salt, pepper, and garlic powder. Place drumsticks into ungreased air fryer basket. 2. Adjust the temperature to 200°C and air fry for 25 minutes, turning drumsticks halfway through cooking. Drumsticks will be golden and have an internal temperature of at least 76°C when done. 3. Transfer drumsticks to a large serving dish. Pour butter over drumsticks, and sprinkle with Parmesan and parsley. Serve warm.

Bacon-Wrapped Stuffed Chicken Breasts

Prep time: 15 minutes | Cook time: 30 minutes | Serves 4

- ◆ 80 g chopped frozen spinach, thawed and squeezed dry
- ◆ 55 g cream cheese, softened
- ◆ 20 g grated Parmesan cheese
- ◆ 1 jalapeño, seeded and chopped
- ◆ ½ teaspoon kosher salt
- ◆ 1 teaspoon black pepper
- ◆ 2 large boneless, skinless chicken breasts, butterflied and pounded to ½-inch thickness
- ◆ 4 teaspoons salt-free Cajun seasoning
- ◆ 6 slices bacon

1. In a small bowl, combine the spinach, cream cheese, Parmesan cheese, jalapeño, salt, and pepper. Stir until well combined. 2. Place the butterflied chicken breasts on a flat surface. Spread the cream cheese mixture evenly across each piece of chicken. Starting with the narrow end, roll up each chicken breast, ensuring the filling stays inside. Season chicken with the Cajun seasoning, patting it in to ensure it sticks to the meat. 3. Wrap each breast in 3 slices of bacon. Place in the air fryer basket. Set the air fryer to 180°C for 30 minutes. Use a meat thermometer to ensure the chicken has reached an internal temperature of 76°C. 4. Let the chicken stand 5 minutes before slicing each rolled-up breast in half to serve.

Golden Tenders

Prep time: 10 minutes | Cook time: 15 minutes | Serves 4

- ◆ 60 g panko bread crumbs
- ◆ 1 tablespoon paprika
- ◆ ½ teaspoon salt
- ◆ ¼ teaspoon freshly ground black pepper
- ◆ 16 chicken tenders
- ◆ 115 g mayonnaise
- ◆ Olive oil spray

1. In a medium bowl, stir together the panko, paprika, salt, and pepper. 2. In a large bowl, toss together the chicken tenders and mayonnaise to coat. Transfer the coated chicken pieces to the bowl of seasoned panko and dredge to coat thoroughly. Press the coating onto the chicken with your fingers. 3. Insert the crisper plate into the basket and the basket into the unit. Preheat the unit by selecting AIR FRY, setting the temperature to 180°C, and setting the time to 3 minutes. Select START/STOP to begin. 4. Once the unit is preheated, place a parchment paper liner into the basket. Place the chicken into the basket and spray it with olive oil. 5. Select AIR FRY, set the temperature to 180°C, and set the time to 15 minutes. Select START/STOP to begin. 6. When the cooking is complete, the tenders will be golden brown and a food thermometer inserted into the chicken should register 76°C. For more even browning, remove the basket halfway through cooking and flip the tenders. Give them an extra spray of olive oil and reinsert the basket to resume cooking. This ensures they are crispy and brown all over. 7. When the cooking is complete, serve.

CHAPTER 7 Snacks and Starters

Onion Pakoras

Prep time: 30 minutes | Cook time: 10 minutes per batch | Serves 2

◆ two medium-sized brown or white onions, sliced (475 g)
◆ 30 g finely chopped fresh coriander
◆ 2 tablespoons mixed vegetables oil
◆ 1 tablespoon gram flour
◆ 1 tablespoon rice flour, or 2 tablespoons gram flour
◆ 1 teaspoon turmeric powder
◆ 1 teaspoon cumin seeds
◆ 1 teaspoon rock salt
◆ ½ teaspoon cayenne pepper
◆ mixed vegetables oil spray

1. In a large bowl, combine the onions, coriander, oil, gram flour, rice flour, turmeric, cumin seeds, salt, and cayenne. Stir to combine. Cover and let stand for 30 minutes or up to overnight. (This allows the onions to release moisture, creating a batter.) Mix well before using. 2. Spray the air fryer basket generously with mixed vegetables oil spray. Drop half of the batter in 6 heaped tablespoons into the basket. Set the air fryer to 180°C for 8 minutes. Carefully turn the pakoras over and spray with oil spray. Set the air fryer for 2 minutes, or until the batter is fully cooked and crisp. 3. Repeat with remaining batter to make 6 more pakoras, checking at 6 minutes for degree of doneness. Serve hot.

Homemade Sweet Potato Chips

Prep time: 5 minutes | Cook time: 15 minutes | Serves 2

◆ 1 large sweet potato, sliced thin
◆ ⅛ teaspoon salt
◆ 2 tablespoons olive oil

1. Preheat the air fryer to 190°C. 2. In a small bowl, toss the sweet potatoes, salt, and olive oil together until the potatoes are well coated. 3. Put the sweet potato slices into the air fryer and spread them out in a single layer. 4. Fry for 10 minutes. Stir, then air fry for 3 to 5 minutes more, or until the crisps reach the preferred level of crispiness.

Turkey Burger Sliders

Prep time: 10 minutes | Cook time: 5 to 7 minutes | Makes 8 sliders

◆ 450 g finely chopped turkey
◆ ¼ teaspoon curry powder
◆ 1 teaspoon Hoisin sauce
◆ ½ teaspoon salt
◆ 8 mini rolls
◆ 60 g thinly sliced red onions
◆ 60 g slivered green or red pepper
◆ 100 g fresh diced pineapple
◆ Light soft white cheese

1. Combine turkey, curry powder, Hoisin sauce, and salt and mix together well. 2. Shape turkey mixture into 8 small burger patties. 3. Place burger patties in air fryer basket and air fry at 180°C for 5 to 7 minutes, until burger patties are well done, and the juices are clear. 4. Place each patty on the bottom half of a slider roll and top with onions, peppers, and pineapple. Spread the remaining bun halves with soft white cheese to taste, place on top, and serve.

Crispy Cajun Fresh Dill Gherkin Chips

Prep time: 5 minutes | Cook time: 10 minutes | Makes 16 slices

◆ 30 g plain flour
◆ 42 g panko breadcrumbs
◆ 1 large egg, beaten
◆ 2 teaspoons Cajun seasoning
◆ 2 large fresh dill pickled cucumbers, sliced into 8 rounds each
◆ Cooking spray

1. Preheat the air fryer to 200°C. 2. Place the plain flour, panko breadcrumbs, and egg into 3 separate shallow dishes, then stir the Cajun seasoning into the flour. 3. Dredge each gherkin chip in the flour mixture, then the egg, and finally the breadcrumbs. Shake off any excess, then place each coated gherkin chip on a plate. 4. Spritz the air fryer basket with cooking spray, then place 8 gherkin crisps in the basket and air fry for 5 minutes, or

until crispy and golden. Repeat this process with the remaining gherkin chips. 5. Remove the crisps and allow to slightly cool on a a wire rack before serving.

Bruschetta with Basil Pesto

Prep time: 10 minutes | Cook time: 5 to 11 minutes | Serves 4

- ◆ 8 slices French bread, ½ inch thick
- ◆ 2 tablespoons softened butter
- ◆ 120 g shredded mozzarella cheese cheese
- ◆ 120 g basil pesto
- ◆ 240 g chopped cherry tomatoes
- ◆ 2 spring onions, thinly sliced

1. Preheat the air fryer to 180ºC. 2. Spread the bread with the butter and place butter-side up in the air fryer basket. Bake for 3 to 5 minutes, or until the bread is light golden. 3. Remove the bread from the basket and top each piece with some of the cheese. Return to the basket in 2 batches and bake for 1 to 3 minutes, or until the cheese melts. 4. Meanwhile, combine the pesto, tomatoes, and spring onions in a small bowl. 5. When the cheese has melted, remove the bread from the air fryer and place on a serving plate. Top each slice with some of the pesto mixture and serve.

Jalapeño Poppers

Prep time: 10 minutes | Cook time: 20 minutes | Serves 4

- ◆ Oil, for spraying
- ◆ 227 g soft white cheese
- ◆ 177 ml gluten-free breadcrumbs, divided
- ◆ 2 tablespoons chopped fresh parsley
- ◆ ½ teaspoon granulated garlic
- ◆ ½ teaspoon salt
- ◆ 10 red chillis, halved and seeded

1. Line the air fryer basket with parchment and spray lightly with oil. 2. In a medium bowl, mix together the soft white cheese, half of the breadcrumbs, the parsley, garlic, and salt. 3. Spoon the mixture into the jalapeño halves. Gently press the stuffed jalapeños in the remaining breadcrumbs. 4. Place the stuffed jalapeños in the prepared basket. 5. Air fry at 188ºC for 20 minutes, or until the cheese is melted and the breadcrumbs are crisp and golden brown.

Air Fried Pot Stickers

Prep time: 10 minutes | Cook time: 18 to 20 minutes |

Makes 30 pot stickers

- ◆ 35 g finely chopped cabbage
- ◆ 30 g finely chopped red pepper
- ◆ 2 spring onions, finely chopped
- ◆ 1 egg, beaten
- ◆ 2 tablespoons cocktail sauce
- ◆ 2 teaspoons low-salt soy sauce
- ◆ 30 wonton wrappers
- ◆ 1 tablespoon water, for brushing the wrappers

1. Preheat the air fryer to 180ºC. 2. In a small bowl, combine the cabbage, pepper, spring onions, egg, cocktail sauce, and soy sauce, and mix well. 3. Put about 1 teaspoon of the mixture in the centre of each wonton wrapper. Fold the wrapper in half, covering the filling; dampen the edges with water, and seal. You tin crimp the edges of the wrapper with your fingers, so they look like the pot stickers you get in restaurants. Brush them with water. 4. Place the pot stickers in the air fryer basket and air fry in 2 batches for 9 to 10 minutes, or until the pot stickers are hot and the bottoms are lightly browned. 5. Serve hot.

Spicy Chicken Bites

Prep time: 10 minutes | Cook time: 10 to 12 minutes | Makes 30 bites

- ◆ 227 g boneless and skinless chicken thighs, cut into 30 pieces
- ◆ ¼ teaspoon rock salt
- ◆ 2 tablespoons hot sauce
- ◆ Cooking spray

1. Preheat the air fryer to 200ºC. 2. Spray the air fryer basket with cooking spray and season the chicken bites with the rock salt, then place in the basket and air fry for 10 to 12 minutes or until crispy. 3. While the chicken bites cook, pour the hot sauce into a large bowl. 4. Remove the bites and add to the sauce bowl, tossing to coat. Serve warm.

Bacon-Wrapped A Pickled Gherkin Spear

Prep time: 10 minutes | Cook time: 8 minutes | Serves 4

- ◆ 8 to 12 slices bacon
- ◆ 60 g soft white cheese
- ◆ 40 g shredded mozzarella cheese cheese
- ◆ 8 fresh dill a pickled gherkin spears
- ◆ 120 ml ranch dressing

1. Lay the bacon slices on a flat surface. In a medium-sized bowl, combine the soft white cheese and mozzarella cheese. stir until thoroughly combined. Spread the cheese mixture over the bacon slices. 2. Place a a pickled gherkin spear on a bacon slice and roll the bacon around the gherkin in a spiral, ensuring the gherkin is fully covered. (You may need to use more than one slice of bacon per gherkin to fully cover the spear.) Fold in the ends to ensure the bacon stays put. Repeat to wrap all the pickled cucumbers. 3. Place the wrapped pickled cucumbers in the air fryer basket in a single layer. Set the air fryer to 200°C for 8 minutes, or until the bacon is fully cooked and crisp on the edges. 4. Serve the a pickled gherkin spears with ranch dressing on the side.

Prawns Egg Rolls

Prep time: 15 minutes | Cook time: 10 minutes per batch | Serves 4

◆ 1 tablespoon mixed vegetables oil
◆ ½ head green or savoy cabbage, finely shredded
◆ 90 g grated carrots
◆ 240 ml canned bean sprouts, drained
◆ 1 tablespoon soy sauce
◆ ½ teaspoon sugar
◆ 1 teaspoon sesame oil
◆ 60 ml hoisin sauce
◆ Freshly ground black pepper, to taste
◆ 454 g cooked prawns, diced
◆ 30 g spring onions
◆ 8 egg roll wrappers (or use spring roll pastry)
◆ mixed vegetables oil
◆ Duck sauce

1. Preheat a large sauté pan over medium-high heat. Add the oil and cook the cabbage, carrots and bean sprouts until they start to wilt, about 3 minutes. Add the soy sauce, sugar, sesame oil, hoisin sauce and black pepper. Sauté for a few more minutes. Stir in the prawns and spring onions and cook until the mixed vegetables are just tender. Transfer the mixture to a colander in a bowl to cool. Press or squeeze out any excess water from the filling so that you don't end up with soggy egg rolls. 2. Make the egg rolls: Place the egg roll wrappers on a flat surface with one of the points facing towards you so they look like diamonds. Dividing the filling evenly between the eight wrappers, spoon the mixture onto the centre of the egg roll wrappers. Spread the filling across the centre of the wrappers from the left corner to

the right corner but leave 2 inches from each corner empty. Brush the empty sides of the wrapper with a little water. Fold the bottom corner of the wrapper tightly up over the filling, trying to avoid making any air pockets. Fold the left corner in toward the centre and then the right corner toward the centre. It should now look like an packet. Tightly roll the egg roll from the bottom to the top open corner. Press to seal the egg roll together, brushing with a little extra water if need be. Repeat this technique with all 8 egg rolls. 3. Preheat the air fryer to 190°C. 4. Spray or brush all sides of the egg rolls with mixed vegetables oil. Air fry four egg rolls at a time for 10 minutes, turning them over halfway through the cooking time. 5. Serve hot with duck sauce or your favourite dipping sauce.

Cheese-Stuffed Blooming Onion

Prep time: 10 minutes | Cook time: 15 minutes | Serves 2

◆ 1 large brown onion (397 g)
◆ 1 tablespoon olive oil
◆ Rock salt and freshly ground black pepper, to taste
◆ 18 g plus 2 tablespoons panko breadcrumbs
◆ 22 g grated Parmesan cheese
◆ 3 tablespoons mayonnaise
◆ 1 tablespoon fresh lemon juice
◆ 1 tablespoon chopped fresh flat-leaf parsley parsley
◆ 2 teaspoons wholemeal Dijon mustard
◆ 1 garlic clove, minced

1. Place the onion on a cutting board and trim the top off and peel off the outer skin. Turn the onion upside down and use a paring knife, cut vertical slits halfway through the onion at ½-inch intervals around the onion, keeping the root intact. When you turn the onion right side up, it should open up like the petals of a flower. Drizzle the cut sides of the onion with the olive oil and season with salt and pepper. Place petal-side up in the air fryer and air fry at 180°C for 10 minutes. 2. Meanwhile, in a bowl, stir together the panko, Parmesan, mayonnaise, lemon juice, parsley, mustard, and garlic until incorporated into a smooth paste. 3. Remove the onion from the fryer and stuff the paste all over and in between the onion "petals." Return the onion to the air fryer and air fry at 190°C until the onion is tender in the centre and the bread crumb mixture is golden, about 5 minutes. Remove the onion from the air fryer, transfer to a plate, and serve hot.

Kale Crisps with Tex-Mex Dip

Prep time: 10 minutes | Cook time: 5 to 6 minutes |
Serves 8

◆ 240 ml Greek yoghurt
◆ 1 tablespoon chilli powder
◆ 80 ml low-salt salsa, well drained
◆ 1 bunch curly kale
◆ 1 teaspoon olive oil
◆ ¼ teaspoon coarse sea salt

1. In a small bowl, combine the yoghurt, chilli powder, and drained salsa; refrigerate. 2. Rinse the kale thoroughly, and pat dry. Remove the stems and ribs from the kale, using a sharp knife. Cut or tear the leaves into 3-inch pieces. 3. Toss the kale with the olive oil in a large bowl. 4. Air fry the kale in small batches at 200°C until the leaves are crisp. This should take 5 to 6 minutes. Shake the basket once during cooking time. 5. As you remove the kale chips, sprinkle them with a bit of the sea salt. 6. When all of the kale crisps are done, serve with the dip.

Fried Artichoke Hearts

Prep time: 10 minutes | Cook time: 12 minutes | Serves
10

◆ Oil, for spraying
◆ 3 (397 g) tins quartered artichokes, drained and patted dry
◆ 120 ml mayonnaise
◆ 180 g panko breadcrumbs
◆ 50 g grated Parmesan cheese
◆ Salt and freshly ground black pepper, to taste

1. Line the air fryer basket with baking paper and spray lightly with oil. 2. Place the artichokes on a plate. Put the mayonnaise and breadcrumbs in separate bowls. 3. Working one at a time, dredge each artichoke heart in the mayonnaise, then in the breadcrumbs to cover. 4. Place the artichokes in the prepared basket. You may need to work in batches, depending on the size of your air fryer. 5. Air fry at 190°C for 10 to 12 minutes, or until crispy and golden. 6. Sprinkle with the Parmesan cheese and season with salt and black pepper. Serve immediately.

Cheese Drops

Prep time: 15 minutes | Cook time: 10 minutes per
batch | Serves 8

◆ 90 g plain flour
◆ ½ teaspoon rock salt
◆ ¼ teaspoon cayenne pepper
◆ ¼ teaspoon smoked paprika
◆ ¼ teaspoon black pepper
◆ a dash of garlic powder (optional)
◆ 57 g butter, softened
◆ 100 g grated extra mature cheddar cheese, at room temperature
◆ Olive oil spray

1. In a small bowl, combine the flour, salt, cayenne, paprika, pepper, and garlic powder, if using. 2. Using a food processor, cream the butter and cheese until smooth. Gently add the seasoned flour and process until the dough is well combined, smooth, and no longer sticky. (Or make the dough in a stand mixer fitted with the paddle attachment: Cream the butter and cheese at medium speed until smooth, then add the seasoned flour and beat at low speed until smooth.) 3. Divide the dough into 32 pieces of equal size. On a lightly floured surface, roll each piece into a small ball. 4. Spray the air fryer basket with oil spray. Arrange 16 cheese drops in the basket. Set the air fryer to 160°C for 10 minutes, or until drops are just starting to brown. Transfer to a a wire rack. Repeat with remaining dough, checking for degree of doneness at 8 minutes. 5. Cool the cheese drops completely on the a wire rack. Store in an airtight container until ready to serve, or up to 1 or 2 days.

Lemon Prawns with Garlic Olive Oil

Prep time: 5 minutes | Cook time: 6 minutes | Serves 4

◆ 340 g medium prawns, cleaned and deveined
◆ 60 ml plus 2 tablespoons olive oil, divided
◆ Juice of ½ lemon
◆ 3 garlic cloves, minced and divided
◆ ½ teaspoon salt
◆ ¼ teaspoon red pepper flakes
◆ Lemon wedges, for serving (optional)
◆ Marinara sauce, for dipping (optional)

1. Preheat the air fryer to 190°C. 2. In a large bowl, combine the prawns with 2 tablespoons of the olive oil, as well as the lemon juice, ⅓ of the minced garlic, salt, and red pepper flakes. Toss to coat the prawns well. 3. In a small ramekin, combine the remaining 60 ml of olive oil and the remaining minced garlic. 4. Tear off a 12-by-12-inch sheet of aluminium foil. Pour the prawns into the centre of the foil, then fold the sides up and crimp the edges so that it forms an aluminium foil bowl that is

open on top. Place this packet into the air fryer basket. 5. Roast the prawns for 4 minutes, then open the air fryer and place the ramekin with oil and garlic in the basket beside the prawns packet. Cook for 2 more minutes. 6. Transfer the prawns on a serving plate or platter with the ramekin of garlic olive oil on the side for dipping. You may also serve with lemon wedges and marinara sauce, if desired.

Prawns Pirogues

Prep time: 15 minutes | Cook time: 4 to 5 minutes | Serves 8

◆   340 g small, peeled, and deveined raw prawns

◆   85 g soft white cheese, at room temperature

◆   2 tablespoons natural yoghurt

◆   1 teaspoon lemon juice

◆   1 teaspoon dried fresh dill, crushed

◆   Salt, to taste

◆   4 small English cucumbers, each approximately 6 inches long

1. Pour 4 tablespoons water in bottom of air fryer drawer. 2. Place prawns in air fryer basket in single layer and air fry at 200ºC for 4 to 5 minutes, just until done. Watch carefully because prawns cooks quickly, and overcooking makes it tough. 3. Chop prawns into small pieces, no larger than ½ inch. Refrigerate while mixing the remaining ingredients. 4. With a fork, mash and whip the soft white cheese until smooth. 5. Stir in the yoghurt and beat until smooth. Stir in lemon juice, fresh dill, and chopped prawns. 6. Taste for seasoning. If needed, add ¼ to ½ teaspoon salt to suit your taste. 7. Store in refrigerator until serving time. 8. When ready to serve, wash and dry cucumbers and split them lengthwise. Scoop out the seeds and turn cucumbers upside down on kitchen roll to drain for 10 minutes. 9. Just before filling, wipe centres of cucumbers dry. Spoon the prawns mixture into the pirogues and cut in half crosswise. Serve immediately.

Goat Cheese and Garlic Crostini

Prep time: 3 minutes | Cook time: 5 minutes | Serves 4

◆   1 wholemeal baguette

◆   60 ml olive oil

◆   2 garlic cloves, minced

◆   113 g goat cheese

◆   2 tablespoons fresh basil, minced

1. Preheat the air fryer to 190ºC. 2. Cut the baguette into ½-inch-thick slices. 3. In a small bowl, mix together the olive oil and garlic, then brush it over one side of each slice of bread. 4. Place the olive-oil-coated bread in a single layer in the air fryer basket and bake for 5 minutes. 5. Meanwhile, in a small bowl, mix together the goat cheese and basil. 6. Remove the toast from the air fryer, then spread a thin layer of the goat cheese mixture over the top of each piece and serve.

Banger Balls with Cheese

Prep time: 10 minutes | Cook time: 10 to 11 minutes | Serves 8

◆   340 g mild banger meat

◆   177 g baking mix

◆   120 g shredded mild Cheddar cheese

◆   85 g soft white cheese, at room temperature

◆   1 to 2 tablespoons olive oil

1. Preheat the air fryer to 160ºC. Line the air fryer basket with baking paper paper. 2. Mix together the ground banger, baking mix, Cheddar cheese, and soft white cheese in a large bowl and stir to incorporate. 3. Divide the banger mixture into 16 equal portions and roll them into 1-inch balls with your hands. 4. Arrange the banger balls on the baking paper, leaving space between each ball. You may need to work in batches to avoid overcrowding. 5. Brush the banger balls with the olive oil. Bake for 10 to 11 minutes, shaking the basket halfway through, or until the balls are firm and lightly browned on both sides. 6. Remove from the basket to a plate and repeat with the remaining balls. 7. Serve warm.

Hasselback Potatoes

Prep time: 5 minutes | Cook time: 50 minutes | Serves 4

◆   4 russet or Maris Piper potatoes, peeled

◆   Salt and freshly ground black pepper, to taste

◆   60 g grated Parmesan cheese

◆   Cooking spray

1. Preheat the air fryer to 200ºC 2.Spray the air fryer basket lightly with cooking spray 3.Make thin parallel cuts into each potato, ⅛-inch to ¼-inch apart, stopping at about ½ of the way through 4.The potato needs to stay intact along the bottom 5.Spray the potatoes with cooking spray and use the hands or a silicone brush to completely coat the potatoes lightly in oil 6.Put the potatoes, sliced side up, in the air fryer basket in a single layer 7.Leave a little room between each potato

8.Sprinkle the potatoes lightly with salt and black pepper 9.Air fry for 20 minutes 10.Reposition the potatoes and spritz lightly with cooking spray again 11.Air fry until the potatoes are fork-tender and crispy and browned, another 20 to 30 minutes 12.Sprinkle the potatoes with Parmesan cheese and serve.

Crispy Green Tomatoes with Horseradish

Prep time: 18 minutes | Cook time: 10 to 15 minutes | Serves 4

- ◆ 2 eggs
- ◆ 60 ml buttermilk
- ◆ 55 g breadcrumbs
- ◆ 75 g cornmeal
- ◆ ¼ teaspoon salt
- ◆ 680 g firm green tomatoes, cut into ¼-inch slices
- ◆ Cooking spray
- ◆ Horseradish Sauce:
- ◆ 60 ml soured cream
- ◆ 60 ml mayonnaise
- ◆ 2 teaspoons prepared horseradish
- ◆ ½ teaspoon lemon juice
- ◆ ½ teaspoon Worcestershire sauce
- ◆ ⅛ teaspoon black pepper

1. Preheat air fryer to 200°C. Spritz the air fryer basket with cooking spray. 2. In a small bowl, whisk together all the ingredients for the horseradish sauce until smooth. Set aside. 3. In a shallow dish, beat the eggs and buttermilk. 4. In a separate shallow dish, thoroughly combine the breadcrumbs, cornmeal, and salt. 5. Dredge the tomato slices, one at a time, in the egg mixture, then roll in the bread crumb mixture until evenly coated. 6. Working in batches, place the tomato slices in the air fryer basket in a single layer. Spray them with cooking spray. 7. Air fry for 10 to 15 minutes, flipping the slices halfway through, or until the tomato slices are nicely browned and crisp. 8. Remove from the basket to a platter and repeat with the remaining tomato slices. 9. Serve drizzled with the prepared horseradish sauce.

CHAPTER 8 Vegetables and Sides

Spiced Butternut Marrow

Prep time: 10 minutes | Cook time: 15 minutes | Serves 4

◆ 600 g 1-inch-cubed butternut marrow

◆ 2 tablespoons vegetable oil

◆ 1 to 2 tablespoons brown sugar

◆ 1 teaspoon Chinese five-spice powder

1. In a medium bowl, combine the marrow, oil, sugar, and five-spice powder. Toss to coat. 2. Place the marrow in the air fryer basket. Set the air fryer to 200°C for 15 minutes or until tender.

Golden Garlicky Mushrooms

Prep time: 10 minutes | Cook time: 10 minutes | Serves 4

◆ 6 small mushrooms

◆ 1 tablespoon bread crumbs

◆ 1 tablespoon olive oil

◆ 30 g onion, peeled and diced

◆ 1 teaspoon parsley

◆ 1 teaspoon garlic purée

◆ Salt and ground black pepper, to taste

1. Preheat the air fryer to 180°C. 2. Combine the bread crumbs, oil, onion, parsley, salt, pepper and garlic in a bowl. Cut out the mushrooms' stalks and stuff each cap with the crumb mixture. 3. Air fry in the air fryer for 10 minutes. 4. Serve hot.

Five-Spice Roasted Sweet Potatoes

Prep time: 10 minutes | Cook time: 12 minutes | Serves 4

◆ ½ teaspoon ground cinnamon

◆ ¼ teaspoon ground cumin

◆ ¼ teaspoon paprika

◆ 1 teaspoon chilli powder

◆ ⅛ teaspoon turmeric

◆ ½ teaspoon salt (optional)

◆ Freshly ground black pepper, to taste

◆ 2 large sweet potatoes, peeled and cut into ¾-inch cubes

◆ 1 tablespoon olive oil

1. In a large bowl, mix together cinnamon, cumin, paprika, chilli powder, turmeric, salt, and pepper to taste. 2. Add potatoes and stir well. 3. Drizzle the seasoned potatoes with the olive oil and stir until evenly coated. 4. Place seasoned potatoes in a baking pan or an ovenproof dish that fits inside your air fryer basket. 5. Cook for 6 minutes at 200°C, stop, and stir well. 6. Cook for an additional 6 minutes.

Spiced Honey-Walnut Carrots

Prep time: 5 minutes | Cook time: 12 minutes | Serves 6

◆ 450 g baby carrots

◆ 2 tablespoons olive oil

◆ 80 g raw honey

◆ ¼ teaspoon ground cinnamon

◆ 25 g black walnuts, chopped

1. Preheat the air fryer to 180°C. 2. In a large bowl, toss the baby carrots with olive oil, honey, and cinnamon until well coated. 3. Pour into the air fryer and roast for 6 minutes. Shake the basket, sprinkle the walnuts on top, and roast for 6 minutes more. 4. Remove the carrots from the air fryer and serve.

Dill-and-Garlic Beetroots

Prep time: 10 minutes | Cook time: 30 minutes | Serves 4

◆ 4 beetroots, cleaned, peeled, and sliced

◆ 1 garlic clove, minced

◆ 2 tablespoons chopped fresh dill

◆ ¼ teaspoon salt

◆ ¼ teaspoon black pepper

◆ 3 tablespoons olive oil

1. Preheat the air fryer to 190°C. 2. In a large bowl, mix together all of the ingredients so the beetroots are well coated with the oil. 3. Pour the beetroot mixture into the air fryer basket, and roast for 15 minutes before stirring, then continue roasting for 15 minutes more.

Lemony Broccoli

Prep time: 10 minutes | Cook time: 9 to 14 minutes per batch | Serves 4

- 1 large head broccoli, rinsed and patted dry
- 2 teaspoons extra-virgin olive oil
- 1 tablespoon freshly squeezed lemon juice
- Olive oil spray

1. Cut off the broccoli florets and separate them. You tin use the stems, too; peel the stems and cut them into 1-inch chunks. 2. Insert the crisper plate into the basket and the basket into the unit. Preheat the unit by selecting AIR ROAST, setting the temperature to 200ºC, and setting the time to 3 minutes. Select START/STOP to begin. 3. In a large bowl, toss together the broccoli, olive oil, and lemon juice until coated. 4. Once the unit is preheated, spray the crisper plate with olive oil. Working in batches, place half the broccoli into the basket. 5. Select AIR ROAST, set the temperature to 200ºC, and set the time to 14 minutes. Select START/STOP to begin. 6. After 5 minutes, remove the basket and shake the broccoli. Reinsert the basket to resume cooking. Check the broccoli after 5 minutes. If it is crisp-tender and slightly brown around the edges, it is done. If not, resume cooking. 7. When the cooking is complete, transfer the broccoli to a serving bowl. Repeat steps 5 and 6 with the remaining broccoli. Serve immediately.

Roasted Brussels Sprouts with Bacon

Prep time: 10 minutes | Cook time: 20 minutes | Serves 4

- 4 slices thick-cut bacon, chopped (about 110 g)
- 450 g Brussels sprouts, halved (or quartered if large)
- Freshly ground black pepper, to taste

1. Preheat the air fryer to 190ºC. 2. Air fry the bacon for 5 minutes, shaking the basket once or twice during the cooking time. 3. Add the Brussels sprouts to the basket and drizzle a little bacon fat from the bottom of the air fryer drawer into the basket. Toss the sprouts to coat with the bacon fat. Air fry for an additional 15 minutes, or until the Brussels sprouts are tender to a knifepoint. 4. Season with freshly ground black pepper.

Butternut Marrow Croquettes

Prep time: 5 minutes | Cook time: 17 minutes | Serves 4

- ⅓ butternut marrow, peeled and grated
- 40 g plain flour
- 2 eggs, whisked

- 4 cloves garlic, minced
- 1½ tablespoons olive oil
- 1 teaspoon fine sea salt
- ⅓ teaspoon freshly ground black pepper, or more to taste
- ⅓ teaspoon dried sage
- A pinch of ground allspice

1. Preheat the air fryer to 170ºC. Line the air fryer basket with parchment paper. 2. In a mixing bowl, stir together all the ingredients until well combined. 3. Make the marrow croquettes: Use a small biscuit scoop to drop tablespoonfuls of the marrow mixture onto a lightly floured surface and shape into balls with your hands. Transfer them to the air fryer basket. 4. Air fry for 17 minutes until the marrow croquettes are golden brown. 5. Remove from the basket to a plate and serve warm.

Stuffed Red Peppers with Herbed Ricotta and Tomatoes

Prep time: 10 minutes | Cook time: 20 minutes | Serves 4

- 2 red peppers
- 250 g cooked brown rice
- 2 plum tomatoes, diced
- 1 garlic clove, minced
- ¼ teaspoon salt
- ¼ teaspoon black pepper
- 115 g ricotta
- 3 tablespoons fresh basil, chopped
- 3 tablespoons fresh oregano, chopped
- 20 g shredded Parmesan, for topping

1. Preheat the air fryer to 180ºC. 2. Cut the peppers in half and remove the seeds and stem. 3. In a medium bowl, combine the brown rice, tomatoes, garlic, salt, and pepper. 4. Distribute the rice filling evenly among the four pepper halves. 5. In a small bowl, combine the ricotta, basil, and oregano. Put the herbed cheese over the top of the rice mixture in each pepper. 6. Place the peppers into the air fryer and roast for 20 minutes. 7. Remove and serve with shredded Parmesan on top.

Green Peas with Mint

Prep time: 5 minutes | Cook time: 5 minutes | Serves 4

- 75 g shredded lettuce
- 1 (280 g) package frozen green peas, thawed
- 1 tablespoon fresh mint, shredded

- 1 teaspoon melted butter

1. Lay the shredded lettuce in the air fryer basket. 2. Toss together the peas, mint, and melted butter and spoon over the lettuce. 3. Air fry at 180°C for 5 minutes, until peas are warm and lettuce wilts.

Spinach and Cheese Stuffed Tomatoes

Prep time: 20 minutes | Cook time: 15 minutes | Serves 2

- 4 ripe beefsteak tomatoes
- ¾ teaspoon black pepper
- ½ teaspoon coarse sea salt
- 1 (280 g) package frozen chopped spinach, thawed and squeezed dry
- 1 (150 g) package garlic-and-herb Boursin cheese
- 3 tablespoons sour cream
- 45 g finely grated Parmesan cheese

1. Cut the tops off the tomatoes. Using a small spoon, carefully remove and discard the pulp. Season the insides with ½ teaspoon of the black pepper and ¼ teaspoon of the salt. Invert the tomatoes onto paper towels and allow to drain while you make the filling. 2. Meanwhile, in a medium bowl, combine the spinach, Boursin cheese, sour cream, ½ of the Parmesan, and the remaining ¼ teaspoon salt and ¼ teaspoon pepper. Stir until ingredients are well combined. Divide the filling among the tomatoes. Top with the remaining ½ of the Parmesan. 3. Place the tomatoes in the air fryer basket. Set the air fryer to 180°C for 15 minutes, or until the filling is hot.

Chermoula-Roasted Beetroots

Prep time: 15 minutes | Cook time: 25 minutes | Serves 4

- Chermoula:
- 30 g packed fresh coriander leaves
- 15 g packed fresh parsley leaves
- 6 cloves garlic, peeled
- 2 teaspoons smoked paprika
- 2 teaspoons ground cumin
- 1 teaspoon ground coriander
- ½ to 1 teaspoon cayenne pepper
- Pinch crushed saffron (optional)
- 115 g extra-virgin olive oil
- coarse sea salt, to taste
- Beetroots:
- 3 medium beetroots, trimmed, peeled, and cut into 1-inch chunks
- 2 tablespoons chopped fresh coriander
- 2 tablespoons chopped fresh parsley

1. For the chermoula: In a food processor, combine the fresh coriander, parsley, garlic, paprika, cumin, ground coriander, and cayenne. Pulse until coarsely chopped. Add the saffron, if using, and process until combined. With the food processor running, slowly add the olive oil in a steady stream; process until the sauce is uniform. Season to taste with salt. 2. For the beetroots: In a large bowl, drizzle the beetroots with ½ cup of the chermoula, or enough to coat. Arrange the beetroots in the air fryer basket. Set the air fryer to 190°C for 25 to minutes, or until the beetroots are tender. 3. Transfer the beetroots to a serving platter. Sprinkle with chopped coriander and parsley and serve.

Garlicky Zoodles

Prep time: 10 minutes | Cook time: 10 minutes | Serves 4

- 2 large courgette, peeled and spiralized
- 2 large yellow butternut squash, peeled and spiralized
- 1 tablespoon olive oil, divided
- ½ teaspoon rock salt
- 1 garlic clove, whole
- 2 tablespoons fresh basil, chopped
- Cooking spray

1. Preheat the air fryer to 180°C 2.Spritz the air fryer basket with cooking spray 3.Combine the courgette and butternut squash with 1 teaspoon olive oil and salt in a large bowl 4.Toss to coat well 5.Transfer the courgette and butternut squash in the preheated air fryer and add the garlic 6.Air fry for 10 minutes or until tender and fragrant 7.Toss the spiralized courgette and butternut squash halfway through the cooking time 8.Transfer the cooked courgette and butternut squash onto a plate and set aside 9.Remove the garlic from the air fryer and allow to cool for a few minutes 10.Mince the garlic and combine with remaining olive oil in a small bowl 11.Stir to mix well 12.Drizzle the spiralized courgette and butternut squash with garlic oil and sprinkle with basil 13.Toss to serve.

Garlic Herb Radishes

Prep time: 10 minutes | Cook time: 10 minutes | Serves 4

- ◆ 450 g radishes
- ◆ 2 tablespoons unsalted butter, melted
- ◆ ½ teaspoon garlic powder
- ◆ ½ teaspoon dried parsley
- ◆ ¼ teaspoon dried oregano
- ◆ ¼ teaspoon ground black pepper

1. Remove roots from radishes and cut into quarters. 2. In a small bowl, add butter and seasonings. Toss the radishes in the herb butter and place into the air fryer basket. 3. Adjust the temperature to 180°C and set the timer for 10 minutes. 4. Halfway through the cooking time, toss the radishes in the air fryer basket. Continue cooking until edges begin to turn brown. 5. Serve warm.

Parmesan Herb Focaccia Bread

Prep time: 10 minutes | Cook time: 10 minutes | Serves 6

- ◆ 225 g shredded Mozzarella cheese
- ◆ 30 g full-fat cream cheese
- ◆ 95 g blanched finely ground almond flour
- ◆ 40 g ground golden flaxseed
- ◆ 20 g grated Parmesan cheese
- ◆ ½ teaspoon bicarbonate of soda
- ◆ 2 large eggs
- ◆ ½ teaspoon garlic powder
- ◆ ¼ teaspoon dried basil
- ◆ ¼ teaspoon dried rosemary
- ◆ 2 tablespoons salted butter, melted and divided

1. Place Mozzarella, cream cheese, and almond flour into a large microwave-safe bowl and microwave for 1 minute. Add the flaxseed, Parmesan, and bicarbonate of soda and stir until smooth ball forms. If the mixture cools too much, it will be hard to mix. Return to microwave for 10 to 15 seconds to rewarm if necessary. 2. Stir in eggs. You may need to use your hands to get them fully incorporated. Just keep stirring and they will absorb into the dough. 3. Sprinkle dough with garlic powder, basil, and rosemary and knead into dough. Grease a baking pan with 1 tablespoon melted butter. Press the dough evenly into the pan. Place pan into the air fryer basket. 4. Adjust the temperature to 200°C and bake for 10 minutes. 5. At 7 minutes,

cover with foil if bread begins to get too dark. 6. Remove and let cool at least 30 minutes. Drizzle with remaining butter and serve.

Roasted Aubergine

Prep time: 15 minutes | Cook time: 15 minutes | Serves 4

- ◆ 1 large aubergine
- ◆ 2 tablespoons olive oil
- ◆ ¼ teaspoon salt
- ◆ ½ teaspoon garlic powder

1. Remove top and bottom from aubergine. Slice aubergine into ¼-inch-thick round slices. 2. Brush slices with olive oil. Sprinkle with salt and garlic powder. Place aubergine slices into the air fryer basket. 3. Adjust the temperature to 200°C and set the timer for 15 minutes. 4. Serve immediately.

Maize and Coriander Salad

Prep time: 10 minutes | Cook time: 10 minutes | Serves 2

- ◆ 2 ears of maize, shucked (halved crosswise if too large to fit in your air fryer)
- ◆ 1 tablespoon unsalted butter, at room temperature
- ◆ 1 teaspoon chilli powder
- ◆ ¼ teaspoon garlic powder
- ◆ coarse sea salt and freshly ground black pepper, to taste
- ◆ 20 g lightly packed fresh coriander leaves
- ◆ 1 tablespoon sour cream
- ◆ 1 tablespoon mayonnaise
- ◆ 1 teaspoon adobo sauce (from a tin of chipotle peppers in adobo sauce)
- ◆ 2 tablespoons crumbled feta cheese
- ◆ Lime wedges, for serving

1. Brush the maize all over with the butter, then sprinkle with the chilli powder and garlic powder, and season with salt and pepper. Place the maize in the air fryer and air fry at 200°C, turning over halfway through, until the kernels are lightly charred and tender, about 10 minutes. 2. Transfer the ears to a cutting board, let stand 1 minute, then carefully cut the kernels off the cobs and move them to a bowl. Add the coriander leaves and toss to combine (the coriander leaves will wilt slightly). 3. In a small bowl, stir together the sour cream, mayonnaise, and adobo sauce. Divide the maize and coriander among plates and

spoon the adobo dressing over the top. Sprinkle with the feta cheese and serve with lime wedges on the side.

Lemon-Thyme Asparagus

Prep time: 5 minutes | Cook time: 4 to 8 minutes | Serves 4

- ◆ 450 g asparagus, woody ends trimmed off
- ◆ 1 tablespoon avocado oil
- ◆ ½ teaspoon dried thyme or ½ tablespoon chopped fresh thyme
- ◆ Sea salt and freshly ground black pepper, to taste
- ◆ 60 g goat cheese, crumbled
- ◆ Zest and juice of 1 lemon
- ◆ Flaky sea salt, for serving (optional)

1. In a medium bowl, toss together the asparagus, avocado oil, and thyme, and season with sea salt and pepper. 2. Place the asparagus in the air fryer basket in a single layer. Set the air fryer to 200ºC and air fry for 4 to 8 minutes, to your desired doneness. 3. Transfer to a serving platter. Top with the goat cheese, lemon zest, and lemon juice. If desired, season with a pinch of flaky salt.

Spinach and Sweet Pepper Poppers

Prep time: 10 minutes | Cook time: 8 minutes | Makes 16 poppers

- ◆ 110 g cream cheese, softened
- ◆ 20 g chopped fresh spinach leaves
- ◆ ½ teaspoon garlic powder
- ◆ 8 mini sweet peppers, tops removed, seeded, and halved lengthwise

1. In a medium bowl, mix cream cheese, spinach, and garlic powder. Place 1 tablespoon mixture into each sweet pepper half and press down to smooth. 2. Place poppers into ungreased air fryer basket. Adjust the temperature to 200ºC and air fry for 8 minutes. Poppers will be done when cheese is browned on top and peppers are tender-crisp. Serve warm.

Fried Courgette Salad

Prep time: 10 minutes | Cook time: 5 to 7 minutes | Serves 4

- ◆ 2 medium courgette, thinly sliced
- ◆ 5 tablespoons olive oil, divided
- ◆ 15 g chopped fresh parsley
- ◆ 2 tablespoons chopped fresh mint

- ◆ Zest and juice of ½ lemon
- ◆ 1 clove garlic, minced
- ◆ 65 g crumbled feta cheese
- ◆ Freshly ground black pepper, to taste

1. Preheat the air fryer to 200ºC. 2. In a large bowl, toss the courgette slices with 1 tablespoon of the olive oil. 3. Working in batches if necessary, arrange the courgette slices in an even layer in the air fryer basket. Pausing halfway through the cooking time to shake the basket, air fry for 5 to 7 minutes until soft and lightly browned on each side. 4. Meanwhile, in a small bowl, combine the remaining 4 tablespoons olive oil, parsley, mint, lemon zest, lemon juice, and garlic. 5. Arrange the courgette on a plate and drizzle with the dressing. Sprinkle the feta and black pepper on top. Serve warm or at room temperature.

Zesty Fried Asparagus

Prep time: 3 minutes | Cook time: 10 minutes | Serves 4

- ◆ Oil, for spraying
- ◆ 10 to 12 spears asparagus, trimmed
- ◆ 2 tablespoons olive oil
- ◆ 1 tablespoon garlic powder
- ◆ 1 teaspoon chilli powder
- ◆ ½ teaspoon ground cumin
- ◆ ¼ teaspoon salt

1. Line the air fryer basket with parchment and spray lightly with oil. 2. If the asparagus are too long to fit easily in the air fryer, cut them in half. 3. Place the asparagus, olive oil, garlic, chilli powder, cumin, and salt in a zip-top plastic bag, seal, and toss until evenly coated. 4. Place the asparagus in the prepared basket. 5. Roast at 200ºC for 5 minutes, flip, and cook for another 5 minutes, or until bright green and firm but tender.

Burger Bun for One

Prep time: 2 minutes | Cook time: 5 minutes | Serves 1

- ◆ 2 tablespoons salted butter, melted
- ◆ 25 g blanched finely ground almond flour
- ◆ ¼ teaspoon baking powder
- ◆ ⅛ teaspoon apple cider vinegar
- ◆ 1 large egg, whisked

1. Pour butter into an ungreased ramekin. Add flour, baking powder, and vinegar to ramekin and stir until combined. Add egg and stir until batter is mostly smooth. 2. Place ramekin into

air fryer basket. Adjust the temperature to 180ºC and bake for 5 minutes. When done, the centre will be firm and the top slightly browned. Let cool, about 5 minutes, then remove from ramekin and slice in half. Serve.

Easy Greek Briami (Ratatouille)

Prep time: 15 minutes | Cook time: 40 minutes | Serves 6

- 2 Maris Piper potatoes, cubed
- 100 g plum tomatoes, cubed
- 1 aubergine, cubed
- 1 courgette, cubed
- 1 red onion, chopped
- 1 red pepper, chopped
- 2 garlic cloves, minced
- 1 teaspoon dried mint
- 1 teaspoon dried parsley
- 1 teaspoon dried oregano
- ½ teaspoon salt
- ½ teaspoon black pepper
- ¼ teaspoon red pepper flakes
- 80 ml olive oil
- 1 (230 g) tin tomato paste
- 65 ml vegetable stock
- 65 ml water

1. Preheat the air fryer to 160ºC. 2. In a large bowl, combine the potatoes, tomatoes, aubergine, courgette onion, pepper, garlic, mint, parsley, oregano, salt, black pepper, and red pepper flakes. 3. In a small bowl, mix together the olive oil, tomato paste, stock, and water. 4. Pour the oil-and-tomato-paste mixture over the vegetables and toss until everything is coated. 5. Pour the coated vegetables into the air fryer basket in an even layer and roast for 20 minutes. After 20 minutes, stir well and spread out again. Roast for an additional 10 minutes, then repeat the process and cook for another 10 minutes.

CHAPTER 9 Vegetarian Mains

Cauliflower Rice-Stuffed Peppers

Prep time: 10 minutes | Cook time: 15 minutes | Serves 4

- 475 g uncooked cauliflower rice
- 180 g drained canned petite diced tomatoes
- 2 tablespoons olive oil
- 235 g shredded Mozzarella cheese
- ¼ teaspoon salt
- ¼ teaspoon ground black pepper
- 4 medium green peppers, tops removed, seeded

1. In a large bowl, mix all ingredients except peppers. 2.Scoop mixture evenly into peppers. 3.Place peppers into ungreased air fryer basket. 4.Adjust the temperature to 180ºC and air fry for 15 minutes. 5.Peppers will be tender, and cheese will be melted when done. 6.Serve warm.

Air Fryer Veggies with Halloumi

Prep time: 5 minutes | Cook time: 14 minutes | Serves 2

- 2 courgettes, cut into even chunks
- 1 large aubergine, peeled, cut into chunks
- 1 large carrot, cut into chunks
- 170 g halloumi cheese, cubed
- 2 teaspoons olive oil
- Salt and black pepper, to taste
- 1 teaspoon dried mixed herbs

1. Preheat the air fryer to 170ºC. 2.Combine the courgettes, aubergine, carrot, cheese, olive oil, salt, and pepper in a large bowl and toss to coat well. 3.Spread the mixture evenly in the air fryer basket and air fry for 14 minutes until crispy and golden, shaking the basket once during cooking. 4.Serve topped with mixed herbs.

Mediterranean Pan Pizza

Prep time: 5 minutes | Cook time: 8 minutes | Serves 2

- 235 g shredded Mozzarella cheese
- ¼ medium red pepper, seeded and chopped
- 120 g chopped fresh spinach leaves
- 2 tablespoons chopped black olives
- 2 tablespoons crumbled feta cheese

1. Sprinkle Mozzarella into an ungreased round non-stick baking dish in an even layer. 2.Add remaining ingredients on top. 3.Place dish into air fryer basket. 4.Adjust the temperature to 180ºC and bake for 8 minutes, checking halfway through to avoid burning. 5.Top of pizza will be golden brown, and the cheese melted when done. 6.Remove dish from fryer and let cool 5 minutes before slicing and serving.

Super Vegetable Burger

Prep time: 15 minutes | Cook time: 12 minutes | Serves 8

- 230 g cauliflower, steamed and diced, rinsed and drained
- 2 teaspoons coconut oil, melted
- 2 teaspoons minced garlic
- 60 g desiccated coconut
- 120 g oats
- 3 tablespoons flour
- 1 tablespoon flaxseeds plus 3 tablespoons water, divided
- 1 teaspoon mustard powder
- 2 teaspoons thyme
- 2 teaspoons parsley
- 2 teaspoons chives
- Salt and ground black pepper, to taste
- 235 g breadcrumbs

1. Preheat the air fryer to 200ºC. 2.Combine the cauliflower with all the ingredients, except for the breadcrumbs, incorporating everything well. 3.Using the hands, shape 8 equal-sized amounts of the mixture into burger patties. 4.Coat the patties in breadcrumbs before putting them in the air fryer basket in a single layer. 5.Air fry for 12 minutes or until crispy. 6.Serve hot.

Baked Turnip and Courgette

Prep time: 5 minutes | Cook time: 15 to 20 minutes | Serves 4

- 3 turnips, sliced
- 1 large courgette, sliced
- 1 large red onion, cut into rings

- ◆ 2 cloves garlic, crushed
- ◆ 1 tablespoon olive oil
- ◆ Salt and black pepper, to taste

1. Preheat the air fryer to 170ºC. 2.Put the turnips, courgette, red onion, and garlic in a baking pan. 3.Drizzle the olive oil over the top and sprinkle with the salt and pepper. 4.Place the baking pan in the preheated air fryer and bake for 15 to 20 minutes, or until the vegetables are tender. 5.Remove from the basket and serve on a plate.

Aubergine and Courgette Bites

Prep time: 30 minutes | Cook time: 30 minutes | Serves 8

- ◆ 2 teaspoons fresh mint leaves, chopped
- ◆ 1½ teaspoons red pepper chilli flakes
- ◆ 2 tablespoons melted butter
- ◆ 450 g aubergine, peeled and cubed
- ◆ 450 g courgette, peeled and cubed
- ◆ 3 tablespoons olive oil

1. Toss all the above ingredients in a large-sized mixing dish. 2.Roast the aubergine and courgette bites for 30 minutes at 160ºC in your air fryer, turning once or twice. 3.Serve with a homemade dipping sauce.

Lush Summer Rolls

Prep time: 15 minutes | Cook time: 15 minutes | Serves 4

- ◆ 235 g shiitake mushroom, sliced thinly
- ◆ 1 celery stick, chopped
- ◆ 1 medium carrot, shredded
- ◆ ½ teaspoon finely chopped ginger
- ◆ 1 teaspoon sugar
- ◆ 1 tablespoon soy sauce
- ◆ 1 teaspoon Engevita yeast flakes
- ◆ 8 spring roll sheets
- ◆ 1 teaspoon maize starch
- ◆ 2 tablespoons water

1. In a bowl, combine the ginger, soy sauce, Engevita yeast flakes, carrots, celery, mushroom, and sugar. 2.Mix the cornflour and water to create an adhesive for the spring rolls. 3.Scoop a tablespoonful of the vegetable mixture into the middle of the spring roll sheets. 4.Brush the edges of the sheets with the cornflour adhesive and enclose around the filling to

make spring rolls. 5.Preheat the air fryer to 200ºC. 6.When warm, place the rolls inside and air fry for 15 minutes or until crisp. 7.Serve hot.

Basmati Risotto

Prep time: 10 minutes | Cook time: 30 minutes | Serves 2

- ◆ 1 onion, diced
- ◆ 1 small carrot, diced
- ◆ 475 ml vegetable broth, boiling
- ◆ 120 g grated Cheddar cheese
- ◆ 1 clove garlic, minced
- ◆ 180 g long-grain basmati rice
- ◆ 1 tablespoon olive oil
- ◆ 1 tablespoon unsalted butter

1. Preheat the air fryer to 200ºC. 2.Grease a baking tin with oil and stir in the butter, garlic, carrot, and onion. 3.Put the tin in the air fryer and bake for 4 minutes. 4.Pour in the rice and bake for a further 4 minutes, stirring three times throughout the baking time. 5.Turn the temperature down to 160ºC. 6.Add the vegetable broth and give the dish a gentle stir. 7.Bake for 22 minutes, leaving the air fryer uncovered. 8.Pour in the cheese, stir once more and serve.

Roasted Veggie Bowl

Prep time: 10 minutes | Cook time: 15 minutes | Serves 2

- ◆ 235 g broccoli florets
- ◆ 235 g quartered Brussels sprouts
- ◆ 120 g cauliflower florets
- ◆ ¼ medium white onion, peeled and sliced ¼ inch thick
- ◆ ½ medium green pepper, seeded and sliced ¼ inch thick
- ◆ 1 tablespoon coconut oil
- ◆ 2 teaspoons chilli powder
- ◆ ½ teaspoon garlic powder
- ◆ ½ teaspoon cumin

1. Toss all ingredients together in a large bowl until vegetables are fully coated with oil and seasoning. Pour vegetables into the air fryer basket. 2.Adjust the temperature to 180ºC and roast for 15 minutes. 3.Shake two or three times during cooking. 4.Serve warm.

Appendix 1: Recipe Index

Printed in Great Britain
by Amazon